DADDING IT!

ROB KEMP

DADDING IT!

Landmark Moments in Your Life as a Father ... and How to Survive Them

GREEN TREE

LONDON · OXFORD · NEW YORK · NEW DELHI · SYDNEY

GREEN TREE
Bloomsbury Publishing Plc
50 Bedford Square, London, WC1B 3DP, UK

BLOOMSBURY, GREEN TREE and the Green Tree logo are trademarks of
Bloomsbury Publishing Plc
First published in Great Britain 2020
Copyright © Rob Kemp, 2020
Illustrations © Anastasiya Zalevskaya, iStock, 2020
Rob Kemp has asserted his right under the Copyright, Designs and Patents Act,
1988, to be identified as Author of this work

For legal purposes the Acknowledgements on p. 225
constitute an extension of this copyright page

A catalogue record for this book is available from the British Library

Library of Congress Cataloguing-in-Publication data has been applied for

ISBN: HB: 978-1-4729-7345-0; eBook: 978-1-4729-7346-7

2 4 6 8 10 9 7 5 3 1

Typeset in Spectral by Deanta Global Publishing Services, Chennai, India
Printed and bound in Great Britain by CPI Group (UK) Ltd, Croydon CR0 4YY

To find out more about our authors and books visit www.bloomsbury.com
and sign up for our newsletters

*For fathers everywhere who never stop
learning on the job ...*

Contents

Introduction   1

The early years:
Milestones 1–32
1   Love at first sight   4
2   Holding your baby for the
     first time   6
3   Driving your baby home   8
4   Baby acknowledges that
     'you're the daddy'   10
5   Feeding time   12
6   Getting your baby's
     name right   14
7   First baby transporter   16
8   Building a nursery   18
9   The baby visitors   20
10   First public nappy change 22
11   Taking baby out on your
     own   24
12   Raising baby's head   26
13   Father and baby bonding
     sessions   28
14   Baby vomits on you   30
15   First decent night's sleep 32
16   Making a splash at bath
     time   34
17   Baby finds what you've
     been hiding   36
18   Baby gets 'sign language' 38
19   Baby gets to grips with
     you   40
20   When you hear yourself
     speaking in months   42
21   First night out together
     without your baby   44
22   Having a conversation
     that isn't about your baby 46
23   Baby starts to talk ...
     almost   48
24   Having sex again   50
25   Baby teeth   52

26   Baby pressures on marital
     relationship   54
27   Baby responds to its own
     name   56
28   First photos of your baby 58
29   Transition to solids   60
30   First steps   62
31   Taking baby to a pub   64
32   Moments of panic   66

The toddler years:
Milestones 33–52
33   Path to potty training   70
34   Time for baby number two? 72
35   Fit to father more kids?   74
36   Doctor Dad – at-a-glance
     guide to child illnesses   76
37   Writing a will – who should
     raise your kids if you die? 80
38   First-time first aid   82
39   Kids' party time   84
40   First-time tantrums   86
41   First time on a plane   88
42   Reading to your child   90
43   Choosing your first
     family pet   92
44   Finding out that your
     kid's a fussy eater   94
45   Child tortures family pet 96
46   Family member dies   98
47   First time you put your
     kid on a bike   100
48   Screening a babysitter   102
49   Panic that you're not
     cutting it as a parent   104
50   Making more time for
     your kids   106
51   Auditing your essential
     dad skills   108
52   Requesting flexible
     working time   110

The school years:
Milestones 53–69

53 Dad's first day at the school
gate 114
54 Getting to know your
kid's friends 116
55 Helping them overcome
shyness 118
56 Your kid swears for the
first time 120
57 Using and perfecting
your dad joke repertoire 122
58 First time at the match 124
59 Question time 126
60 Picking pocket money 130
61 Your kid makes the
school team 132
62 Civil war among siblings 134
63 Your kid's first phone 136
64 Dad's race exposes the
dad bod 138
65 Summer holiday survival 140
66 Dealing with the school bully 142
67 Parents' evening and
feigning an interest
in your kid's education 144
68 Child gets a bad school report 146
69 Exposed to something
nasty online 148

13 facts on how dads do
things differently 150

The teenager years:
Milestones 70–104

70 Kid dresses 'inappropriately' 154
71 Having 'a chat'. Serious talk
time 156
72 Kid starts coming home late 158
73 Issues around body image 160
74 Putting it all down to
hormones 162
75 Dads and teenage
misbehaviour 164

76 Kid is struggling at school 166
77 Kid comes home drunk 169
78 First stand-up row with
your teenager 170
79 Fixing your kid's 'laziness' 172
80 First time as the dad taxi 174
81 Hosting a teenage party 176
82 Kid caught doing drugs 178
83 Giving them careers advice 180
84 Having to punish your
teenager 182
85 Parental differences 184
86 Meeting your teenager's
'special one' 186
87 Musical differences 188
88 Political awakening 190
89 In the eyes of the law 192
90 Teaching your teen to drive 194
91 Funding student lifestyles 196
92 Further education:
a father's role 198
93 Their gap year of discovery 200
94 Sending your kid off to work 202
95 Child takes over
the family business 204
96 Fond farewell 206
97 Dealing with the empty nest 208
98 Rediscovering life after
the kids have left 210
99 Boomerang kid comes back 212
100 Establishing boundaries
with your adult kids 214
101 Dad's midlife crisis 216
102 Giving them away ... 218
103 From good father to
Godfather 220
104 Dad becomes Grandad 222

Father ahead 224
Acknowledgements 225
Useful resources for dads 226
Source credits 229
Index 230
About the author 232

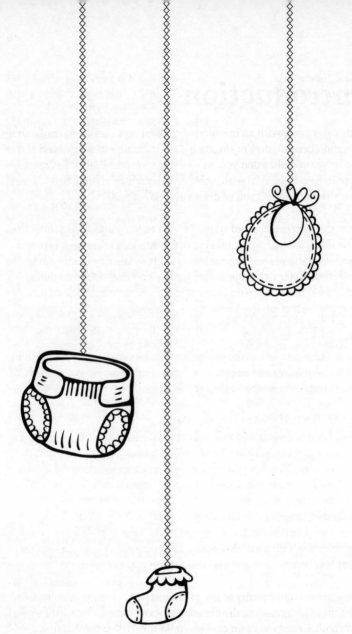

Introduction

Kids don't come with an instruction manual (not that you'd read one if they did). Instead, they're shaped by life-forming milestones and learn-as-they-go mistakes that you, as a modern, responsible father, must be there to help them deal with, solve or at least advise upon pretty much from their birth until you've drawn your last breath.

From their first words and steps through to the start of the school life, those lively teenage years, moving out of home, finding true love and even becoming parents themselves, your role as mentor, role model, adviser, shoulder to cry upon, taxi service and unconditional doting dad is a vital one. You won't always make the right decision or give them the perfect advice. You'll clash with your kids as they strive for independence and you struggle to keep them on the straight and narrow. There will be many moments of pure ecstasy as they surprise you, make you laugh, make you cry and make you proud. There will be moments of anger and anguish – often involving accidental damage to something you treasure – along the way, too.

This book is designed to prepare you for some, if not all, of what lies ahead for many years to come, because no matter if your kid is three months, three years, 13 or 33 and living far away, you're still 'Dad'. It's a job for life ... Yep, bet you hadn't thought about that when the stars all aligned to bring your little wonder into the world!

Remember, though, that all kids are different. They hit different milestones at different stages in their lives – and there's a good chance that they won't hit all of this book's 101 entries. In the event that they do, at least you've now got that instruction manual to hand.

There are of course plenty of pre-birth milestones for the expectant dad to be there for, including the ultrasound scans – there's one at 12 weeks and another at 20 weeks (in case you miss the first one!), your first antenatal class and that moment when she tells you 'it's' time' and your baby is on its way. There are books that highlight these and give advice on what to do before your child comes along – including one by yours truly. But it's only when they finally arrive that the fun and games really begin...

The early years...

Finding your feet, getting to grips with your baby – literally – laying the foundations of fatherhood and discovering new ways to dodge nappy changes ...

Milestone 1

Love at first sight
Age: one day

Meeting your baby for the first time is pretty much the first milestone on the life-long journey through fatherhood. There is, of course, also a good argument to suggest that fatherhood begins long before the birth. For instance, expectant fathers often start developing dad habits – easing up on some of the more reckless elements of their behaviour, becoming more empathetic, and nest-building, before then. Many men also undergo hormonal changes during their partner's pregnancy – a drop in testosterone and oestradiol (a type of oestrogen) – that may trigger a more caring nature in preparation for the new role.

That new caring side may be most evident when your baby is born – being fortunate enough to form the welcoming committee for your new son or daughter can lead to the floodgates opening.

Getting emotional at the birth of your baby is to be expected. But what's not always made clear beforehand is that babies don't always follow the script. Labour wards, hospital suites and even birthing pools can become busy, fraught, hot and bloody at times. It really does pay to watch a birth or two on video if you've never witnessed one before, just to give you a heads-up on what happens when the head's engaged.

Often, the best-laid plans for an immaculate birth get thrown out of the window when your partner goes into labour weeks or months before her due date, or when there are complications with the birth process, or when you find yourself getting a crash course in epidural anaesthesia, ventous extraction or episiotomy. It's a bewildering world for an untrained dad. But in the vast majority of cases, this milestone culminates in a father seeing his new baby for the first time. They may be too tiny to be outside an incubator at first. They may be covered in the goo that giving birth produces. They may be hairy, jaundiced, wrinkling and screaming their head off, but they're yours.

' Dad tales

When Cleo first popped out I think I was in a state of shock. It was 4 a.m., I hadn't slept or eaten since the previous morning and the birth was pretty traumatic. I remember bursting into tears initially while Annie held her, and feeling pretty numb. Nothing sank in properly till a few days later when we finally got her home – first eye contact and finger grabbing were obviously lovely moments. **,**
Nick, father of Cleo

DAD FACTS: You're not alone ...

Around 353,000 babies are born every day, worldwide – that's 255 births each minute. In the UK, at least one baby is born every minute, while 51 are born in India and 8 are born in the USA.
Study conducted by Red Letter Days

Milestone 2

Holding your baby for the first time

Age: one day

> 'Support the neck! Don't let them wriggle! Be gentle! Support
> the neck! Not like that, oh for f*ck's sake give 'em here.'
>
> Anon

I can't attribute that quote to anyone in particular, though it feels fairly familiar to me, but every anxious dad may fear hearing that, especially when you consider that one in five fathers has never held a baby before they first get their hands on their own. Having a hold of your baby at the birth – ideally when you're both topless so you can engage in the much-vaunted skin-on-skin contact – is often the debut moment. But whether it's immediately after the birth or in the days that follow, the technique is straightforward and your fears should be allayed by knowing that babies are remarkably resilient and bounce if dropped as their bones haven't fused yet. Though it's not advisable to test this theory ...

Here's how to handle your baby for the first time ...

Do support the neck ...
You were told. It's because newborns are head-heavy and have been floating around for months on end. They don't have much neck strength yet so you need to use the crook of your elbow to support their head.

... and the rest
With that same arm, use your forearm as a rest and your hand to hold the back, bum and legs.

Close to you

Pull your baby close to your chest with your other arm. It'll make you feel like you've got more purchase and they'll feel as if they're being swaddled. Hold them securely but keeping your body loose – if you're too stiff they won't relax and they'll start to squirm. It's also easier when you're sitting down.

Be prepared

Depending on the moment, you may need to prepare a little:

- A regular birth – the baby is handed to you for some father–baby bonding time, you wipe your hands on your jeans, a towel or scrubs, and then caress said newborn.
- A water birth – Sondico produce a range of all-weather-grip goalie gloves ...

Milestone 3

Driving your baby home

Age: one–four days

All being well, your baby's first moments, minutes and hours out of the womb will have been relatively safe, sterile and secure. They'll hopefully have spent plenty of time with Mum – being fed and bonding – before both are given the all-clear to go home (less than 3 per cent of UK births take place away from a hospital or dedicated birthing centre).

It's unlikely that Mum is going to feel like grabbing the car keys and driving home her newborn and you – though it's not unknown. So, if you are able to drive then you're most likely going to be called upon to taxi your kid home for the very first time ... and certainly not the last. Even if you're picking them up in an actual taxi or minicab you'll still be wise – and on the right side of the law – to ensure they're properly secured.

Safety first

Car seats – including the ones that form part of a 'travel system' buggy set-up – come in the 'age 0' size, which is what you'll need to transport them in. (It'll save on time and embarrassment if you can get familiar with fitting this in the car before your baby is ready to come home.)

Friendly face

Car seats can be fitted to face forwards or backwards. Either way, it's vital to ensure the carrier or seat is supporting their head. If Mum can sit alongside them – it'll be a squeeze in the back of the Lamborghini unfortunately – even better.

Slow start

As keen as you no doubt are to get the new family all back home and comfortable, it pays to ease off the accelerator on this journey, especially bearing in mind the fragile condition of both baby and post-birth mum, when going over speed humps.

Crucially, don't forget to pack an in-car air freshener, in case your newborn decides to 'baptise' the car seat mid-journey – and of course affix the 'Baby On Board' sticker to the rear window.

Milestone 4

Baby acknowledges that 'you're the daddy'
Age: six–eight weeks

One baby will grow differently from the next, but some developmental milestones, such as eye contact, run to form. Typically, you should start getting direct eye contact from your baby at around six–eight weeks old. They're blanking me! What's wrong? OK, it's not unusual for a baby not to initiate eye contact until as late at 12 weeks after you first clamped eyes on them.

It is normal for a baby's eyes to wander or move randomly during the first couple months of life because they are learning how to use their eyes together. Don't fret, you've done nothing to offend them – they're just playing hard to get. One study – published in *Proceedings of the National Academy of Sciences* – showed that newborns are aware of their parents' adoring gaze from just a couple of days old, they've just not got their visual shit together enough to stare back. Another study found that babies prefer to look at faces of people who look directly at them instead of those with an averted gaze. Why the big deal? According to the experts, 'Eye contact indicates that your baby's neurological development is progressing normally.'

As scary as that sounds, the gist of it is that a baby who makes eye contact is showing that she knows what a face is and understands that facial expressions can indicate how a person is feeling. It also makes bonding stronger between parent and child, since it shows you that your baby does know who you are and how important you are in her life.

Do ...

- Go in close. A baby's eyes can only focus on objects that are about 20–37.5cm (8–15in) away – just far enough to see the face of the person holding them.
- Wait until they've been fed. Baby needs to be calm and alert to hold eye contact. Don't try to check this milestone off when they're hungry, distressed or tired, or you'll just piss them off.
- Play peek-a-boo. At about 12 weeks they begin to focus on faces and close objects. You can test how they follow moving objects with their eyes. Playing games that involve you hiding a toy or yourself and suddenly reappearing can encourage them to reach out.

Don't ...

- Flick the nursery light on by surprise just to shock them into looking at you.
- Try moving toys, food or the cat close up and then far away in an attempt to 'train' them.
- Put your prescription glasses on your baby for a photo, at least not on more than one occasion ...

Milestone 5

Feeding time
Age: first year

The opportunity to put food into your kid's mouth can begin pretty much as soon as they're home from hospital – or out of the birthing pool in the front room if you went for the home-birth option.

Breastfeeding from Mum is of course the ideal way to nourish your nipper and should be actively encouraged and supported – but it can be tough going for one parent to bear the brunt of all their needs. Which is where Dad comes in handy. By expressing Mum's milk into bottles via a pump – or filling them with formula (the bottles that is) – dads can take over at feeding times. It can be daunting the first time you do it, but if it's any reassurance, your baby won't tug away at the bottle like the baby goats you'll see being fed at the urban farm a few years from now.

To perfect your feeding technique, take note of the following:

- Keep them close. This can be as much about bonding as giving your baby a bellyful of milk. Hold them close, swaddle them with a warm blanket and ensure any extras – wipes and muslin – are close to hand.
- Learn to latch. This is the part breastfeeding mums often have trouble with: getting a good 'seal' between baby's mouth and boob so they can feed successfully. For dads using a bottle it's easier – in theory. Guide the bottle into their mouth above their tongue. Sometimes, gently pushing their lower lip up with your little finger can help to form a seal.
- Go with the flow. Tilt the bottle so you get a steady flow of milk to the teat without too much air getting in or your baby sucking but not getting any milk. It can take some practice, but since most babies require a feed every one–three hours you're going to get plenty of that …

- Get the wind up. An essential part of the process – burping your baby is something you can do whether you've done the feed or your partner has. For some dads it's a chance to get hands-on, have a chest-to-chest cuddle with your baby, and familiarise yourself with what can sometimes be a messy conclusion to feeding time.
- Take turns at night. Feeding your baby obviously takes pressure off your partner but the pair of you need to determine who's feeding, changing and burping each time – especially at night. When one or both of you is working during the day, the night-time feeds can be especially tough. It may be that one of you can or will do the night shift while the other sleeps. You can swap at weekends until your baby has settled into a longer night-time sleeping and regular feeding routine.

Alternatively, Mum may feed a couple of times early in the night and provide bottles so that dad can take over early in the morning, with the aim of ensuring that you both get at least a half-decent amount of sleep each night.

❛ Dad tales

I've been doing as many nights as I can. Annie expresses in the day for me to do this, which has been crucial, [as has] taking Cleo for a walk after work each night and out as much as I can over the weekend so Annie can have time to herself and to rest. Personally, I've always been able to function fairly well on limited sleep and I think we've chanced upon a fairly "easy-going" baby – she sleeps for six hours at a time, doesn't cry unless she's hungry and only craps every two days. If things continue as they have started we'll be delighted. ❜

Nick, father of Cleo

Milestone 6

Getting your baby's name right
Age: 1–43 days

By law, parents in most of the UK must register their child's birth within 42 days (or 21 days in Scotland) in order to obtain a birth certificate. This may be the first time that you write their name, so it pays to agree on what it is before the ink dries. Baby naming has become an industry in itself with websites, books and even consultants on hand to chip in with worthy advice, which still doesn't stop your kid being one of 15 Isabelles in the same nursery class.

When it comes to choosing a child's name, common sense dictates that it should be something you've no qualms about shouting aloud from the touchline of the school playing field in years to come. Some names can go out of fashion, other more unique ones will help your child stand out online – it's your call as to whether you think that's a positive or not. Go for a name that has great meaning to you both, or maybe celebrates a hero or heroine or which just seems to suit your baby and don't worry if it's not the most original, unique or obscure name either, there are benefits to every moniker:

- Easy-to-pronounce names open doors. Caoimhe or Leuan may work as a nod to an Irish or Welsh ancestor, but calling him or her a plain and simple 'Liam' could help your kid out more in the long run. A New York University study found that people with easier-to-pronounce names – that others have no problem comprehending – often have higher-status positions at work.
- Common kids' names are common for a reason. Again, there's some science behind why your Noahs, Jessicas, Mohammeds and

Sophias still abound. Researchers from Marquette University in the USA discovered that the more common the name, the more popular the name-holder is.

- Prepare for mixed reactions. Throwing an Ivan, Ernest or Cronus into the mix could raise the odd eyebrow at the christening or naming ceremony. Even kids themselves can develop a dislike for their own name – especially if it makes them self-conscious in those formative school years. Don't be shocked if they adapt their own moniker at some point. Also, in Ancient Greek legend Cronus/Kronos killed his own dad. Giving a quirky name to your child as a middle name is much safer and will make for an interesting talking point for them at dinner parties in years to come.

Discuss names you both like, or have a family association, or evoke a fond memory – or that mirror the name of a wealthy relative whose estate could help cover some costs in years to come …

Name your baby for success …

Career	Lawyer	Athlete	Artist	Reality TV star	Politician
Names	Allegra	Jess	J.M.W	Danni	Winston
	Aubyn	Harry	Frida	Dax	Hillary

Milestone 7

First baby transporter
Age: one month

Getting a pram, buggy or multi-functioning travel system can be the first major purchase you make as a new family. Much like a car, you need to consider such factors as budget, brand, lifestyle practicalities and envy potential. Talking to other dads about their first choice of 'chariot' may seem a bit *Top Gear* but it can help uncover any issues you may not have considered.

There are four basic types, from which a million different versions have evolved:

1. The pram. This is your newborn's vehicle, aimed at the youngest end of the market (as in just born up to around six months old). It's usually a parent-facing model providing comfort and space, but which is a bugger to get on to a bus.
2. The pushchair. Aimed at the other end of the age range – geared towards toddler-racers – these are forward-facing sets of wheels, now more fashionably dubbed a 'stroller'. Handy for holidays, they're usually last seen left on the baggage reclaim carousel.
3. The buggy. Different people have different definitions of what a buggy is. For some, it's basically a stroller; for others, it's a full-on travel system. Either way, it's a means of transporting children who can't be arsed to walk.
4. The travel system. A 'combi' vehicle with detachable baby holder that also doubles as a car seat. Multi-facing with additional extras often included – sun shade, 'parcel tray' on the chassis, brakes that work, suspension, etc.

Whatever type you opt for, take note of a few hard-learned rules of buggy buying and pushchair purchase ...

Buy early

If you're going to be taking your newborn baby home from hospital in your own car then buy your baby transport beforehand – especially as the travel system type comes with a removable carrier. This can be used as a car seat, and doubles up as a functional way of carrying your baby around the house when you fear they may be too damp to hold in your hands.

Try before you buy

Poor pushchair posture is a recognised cause of injury in 73 per cent of new parents! Practise your pushing technique, get comfy with the buggy and learn how to adjust it easily and safely before buying.

Practise at home

Don't wait until your screaming, wriggling baby arrives before trying to fold down your new buggy, adjust which way the seat faces, or unpack it from the box. Have some handling practice before they're born and find out where the 'quick release' catches are – learning to use them without turning it into an 'ejector seat' for your baby or a quick way to remove one of your own fingers is a cunning plan.

Measure up

Some stores may let you take a buggy to the car park, fold it down and see if it'll stash away safely in the boot of your car. These stores only exist in baby magazine or website fantasy. Ideally measure the height, width and depth of your boot – then do the same with the buggy. Or else just buy it online and hope baby arrives before the 28-day return policy expires.

Milestone 8

Building a nursery
Age: pre-birth–never getting around to finishing it

Whatever your taste in decor, your own artistic ability or your budget, there are a few distinct elements to a baby's bedroom or nursery that mark it out from any other room in the house. If you're charged with running this 'project' the main practicalities to consider are heating and lighting – your baby shouldn't have its cot in direct sunlight, beside the radiator or in a draft. Beyond that, it's a case of taking your pick from a million options of varying usefulness.

Nursery clobber to consider

Must haves	Might haves	Don't bothers
Cot bed	Clothes hamper	Rocking chair
Changing table or flat-topped cabinet on which to change your baby	Room thermometer	Electric socket covers
Sealable nappy bin	Room fan and window shade	Dangly mobile
Soft toys	Baby sleep monitor	Warm tones night light

Nigel Higgins, founder and writer of the @DIYDaddy blog, also has a few useful tips for fathers on their first expedition into the world of kids' bedroom design and creation:

- Once you have decided on the bedroom that will become the nursery it's important to get the nursery exactly right. By that I mean looking fantastic while also being practical.
- So often I see a nursery that has gone over the top with either pink or blue depending on whether you have a boy or a girl. What I would suggest is using neutral colours and then accessorising with either blue or pink. Remember, this will change eventually into your child's bedroom. Also, always use water-based paints that are non-toxic.
- Black-out blinds are also a brilliant way of helping a baby sleep and keeping a room cool.
- I have found that laminate flooring is perfect because there will be lots of spills and it's really easy to keep clean.
- Finally, don't overclutter the nursery with furniture – you will need lots of room for nappy changing; only start 'accessorising' once you've got used to using the room.

Milestone 9

The baby visitors
Age: one day–one month

Gawpers, well-wishers, nosy neighbours, cold callers, meaningful relatives, meaningless relatives, postnatal care workers, Instagram influencers – all sorts suddenly appear out of the woodwork when there's a new baby to be seen. Dad's role in this whole exhibition and inquest is often one of just policing the crowd and putting the kettle on.

To make the first visits go well, let people know when to come, and when not to come, using social media, texts, etc. – anything that doesn't wake the baby. Try dovetailing visits from those who mean well with your own paternity leave, and limit the time people stay for.

Visiting hours

Who	How long	Activity levels
Close family	60 minutes	Tea, biscuit, hold of baby and photo
Work colleagues	30 minutes	Tea, chat and photo
Pub friends	15 minutes	Photo, sod off

While people are there, you should:

- Accept all offers of help – ironing, making meals, watching baby while the pair of you take a nap. But don't let them tire your baby or your partner out or irritate them any more than family visits normally do.
- Take advantage of the additional company to have a few pics of your new family taken too.
- Consider letting friends and relatives hold the baby. Some new mums aren't always comfortable with this – and not without good reason. Newborns, especially premature babies, are more prone to adult bugs because their immune system really hasn't kicked in yet. If a visitor is unwell – has diarrhoea and vomiting, coughs or flu – then you probably won't want them in the house anyway, but certainly don't let them get close to your baby.

- Smokers are advised to wash their hands before holding babies or avoid holding them at all because of the harmful toxins that can stay in their skin and clothing after smoking.
- Have a 'safe' word, agreed with your partner, to use when she wants visitors to go. When you hear it, start gathering up the tea cups and ushering the clan out of the door mumbling something about 'feeding time' and 'sticking to baby's routine' to chivvy any dawdlers along.

' Dad tales

My wife wanted to put off having visitors for as long as possible. She was exhausted and a bit worried about germs, plus our flat was a mess for the first couple of weeks. When we did have people around it was a bit of a chore settling Charlotte afterwards, but the company was good for us both. '
Mark, father of Charlotte

Double-edged grandparents

It's not only the relationship you have with your partner that changes when you become a dad; the way you interact with your friends and especially your own parents and your in-laws changes, too. Having your child's grandparents on hand to help support you and your partner, to nurture and help raise your child and to be on call as 'mates rates' babysitters, can be very helpful throughout the time your child is at home with you, and beyond, but it can be a mixed blessing. Your child's grandparents have been there before, obviously, and their input can often be helpful – though not all the time. As a new young family you need your own space to find things out for yourself, but if one or both sets of grandparents don't see that too then there can be conflict. Talk it through with your partner – though she may well raise the issue first if she feels that her mother or mother-in-law is interfering too much – and agree to set some boundaries. You're well within your rights to say 'no thanks' or 'time's up', or to politely point out to them that you have your own way of raising your son and daughter and you'd prefer they adhered to it as well. It's about striking a balance – you want and need them, and they should be there to have a relationship with you and their grandchild, but it needs to be on your terms.

Milestone 10

First public nappy change
Age: week one onwards

Expectant parents live in fear of that first major nappy change. Dads-to-be, in particular, will become uneasy at the thought of having to deal with the business end of a baby prior to its arrival. Those same dads are hardly enamoured with the prospect of wiping up poo, smearing on cream and disposing of the dump-filled diaper once their nipper has actually been born either – but it's the fear that's worse than the act itself. That said, there are common tales and graphic images these days that show just how bad baby poo can get.

Knowledge is power

You need to know that your kid's first poo will be nine months' worth of backed-up waste. It's such a landmark achievement that it even comes with its own name: meconium. This usually black, sticky and tar-like turd is actually worse than it smells – cleaning your baby after their debut meconium poo feels a bit like saving a seagull after an oil slick. After that, things can get really messy. Set a template with your first nappy change by covering the surrounding area with an old towel, then perform the following:

- Keep your head back. Removing a baby's nappy and exposing their nether regions to cooler air can trip their personal sprinkler system, potentially giving you a soaking, in your face if the baby's a boy.
- Keep their back flat. Change your baby on a flat, stable surface, ideally with a changing mat between exposed baby's bum and your carpet or changing table.

- Keep your tools to hand. Like a surgeon about to perform an intricate operation, you need to surround yourself with the tools (baby wipes, disposal bags, nappy cream, fresh nappy etc.) *before* you start.
- Keep 'em clean. Clean and dry your baby thoroughly and apply any creams you're using before putting on the fresh nappy.

In the bag

Since you never know when you're going to need it, be sure to pack your dad bag with changing gear whenever you're taking your nipper out alone. Handily, there are also phone apps available that reveal which local stores, coffee shops and pubs have baby changing facilities.

Be aware that babies can go through 60 nappy changes a week – and that they quite often pee or poo within three minutes of waking up from a decent kip. Use this knowledge to wait before changing them ... or else leave them alone with your partner every time you hear them stirring from their slumber.

‘ Dad tales: Nappy shopper

It was in a cafe in a Dunhelm furniture store. He was "stationed" on my lap and about two weeks old! I suddenly felt this warm blob around my leg. Yep, "this is the one". We went to the disabled toilet and I used what seemed like 10 tonnes of wet wipes as it had gone up his back, too. Luckily I've got much better all round at it since! **,**

Han-son, father of Max

Milestone 11

Taking baby out on your own

Age: week two-four

The stark realities of new parenthood hit home in a multitude of different ways – from the sudden shock of sleepless nights to the stealth appearance of the 'dad bod'. But one relatively recent addition to the list of markers that set you apart from non-parents is parental leave – paternity or maternity leave. This is time off from work, when you are paid (to an extent) to look after your baby. That first day of not going into work but instead looking after baby can play havoc with your routine. Instead of the stress-filled commute, banter with colleagues or ear-bashing from the boss, it's just you and a baby. All. Day. Long.

There's plenty of evidence to show that spending time (lots of it) alone with your baby is really important in creating a lasting bond and a healthy family – but it's no walk in the park, except when it is exactly that. This milestone moment does need some forethought on the part of both parents – plus some agreement in advance with employers. The key points to chew over are:

- Days don't come for free – paternity leave isn't time off with full pay. There's a statutory minimum, but depending on your employer you may not get any more than that. With the average cost of raising a child put at £75,000 ($90,000) you may not want to take a pay cut – even for just a fortnight.
- Sharing is caring, but ... Shared parental leave (SPL) is a scheme that enables parents to share up to 52 weeks off between them, as well as up to 39 weeks of statutory shared parental pay. However, research showed that four years after the introduction of SPL, only 1 per cent of men had taken up the opportunity. Finances are still a major stumbling block; one in two dads won't take up parental leave because they earn more money than their partner.

Once you're on paternity leave

If you can work around the finances and take time out in those early days of parenthood, here are a few survival tips to arm yourself with:

- Get out. Weather permitting, head to the coffee shops, libraries or parks – anywhere you can get a bit of adult company, outdoor stimulation and fresh air.
- Work's out. The temptation to check emails and get some work done from home will be high, and at times it will be feasible – but don't make any promises that you will be on call.
- Cook up. Parents will tell you that some days the focus can be so much on your baby's needs that you forget to eat yourself – or else you live off biscuits, like a marooned sailor, for days on end. Bagging up healthy snacks when you have a spare five minutes is one way through this. Cooking extra at mealtimes that you can reheat for lunch the next day is a sound move, too.
- Sleep together. When your baby takes a nap, aim to do the same too – once they're secure in the cot, not next to you on the sofa. Housework and life admin can wait. The priority for parents at home with their baby is to be as fresh, alert and moodiness-free as possible for those precious waking moments. Of course all of this goes out of the window if you have other children …

❛ Dad tale

I've probably always been a bit of a show-off and that has dominated some of my favourite parts of being a parent so far. Strapping her to me and bowling into my local and my office the first times were lovely moments. Similarly, meeting friends and family for the first time, I find myself beaming with pride handing her over. I also really enjoy how many people I'll get chatting to now, out and about in the park, supermarket or pub. People seem very happy to approach to look at, and ask about, Cleo, which is lovely - I don't usually get chatting to people in Tesco when selecting dinner. ❜

Nick, father of Cleo

Milestone 12

Raising baby's head
Age: four months-ish

As you know from countless bollockings, a newborn baby has little control over his or her head because their motor skills and neck muscles are fairly weak at first, and their head must be supported whenever you hold them. However, they'll develop a knack for doing it by around 16 weeks (four months) and have strong enough neck muscles to control movements by six months.

'So bloody what?' I hear you ask. Well, while it seems innocuous enough to those of us capable of nodding, shaking and banging our heads against a brick wall, head control is said to be a foundation for all later movement – sitting up, walking – as well as swallowing food and looking comfy in a highchair. It's a key developmental stage and one to check off the list of 'achievements' you're boring your workmates with. Here are some more facts your friends are doubtless desperate to know:

- By around four months your baby should be able to raise their head to around 45 degrees while lying on their tummy, and to keep it up steadily. (Note – if your baby seems to struggle to lift his or her head up even slightly at three months, mention it at your next doctor visit.)
- One way of helping with the development of the neck muscles is to place your baby on his or her back and then to gently raise them by their hands up to a sitting position, before slowly easing them back down.
- By six months, they should be holding their head steady and able to flex it forwards when they're pulled up into a sitting position. Once your baby can hold their head in line with the rest of their body their neck strength is such that they can be turned to face outwards in the baby carrier.

While they're still wobbly

You don't have to do much to encourage the development of head control, but you do have to be careful until it's well established. Until then:

- Use pillows, or set them on your lap with their back against you, to support them.
- Move them to sit in different spots around your home, so they get a change of scenery.
- Don't leave them propped up unattended – they topple over, which is only really funny once.

Milestone 13

Father and baby bonding sessions
Age: week one onwards

Holding, carrying, cuddling, rocking, feeding, bathing, nappy changing, washing, dressing, nappy changing again, playing with, singing to, chatting with – there are loads of ways dads naturally, instinctively bond with their babies from the start. However, some dads find they take to it a lot more easily than others. The type of bonding that the experts suggest may have greater long-term impact doesn't happen as readily, but that doesn't mean it's difficult to do.

Rub them up
Easy to learn, fun and therapeutic to do, baby massage may seem a bit 'out there' but doing things like actively stroking your baby while naming parts of their body has been shown to help with language development and body awareness.

Go for a dip
Baby swim classes are immense fun and a great way of releasing feel-good hormones in both baby and dad. The warm water, the light and the floating sensation seem to take a baby back to the womb – or maybe they're just happy because they've peed in the pool (do put a special swimming nappy on them). Classes usually begin at around six months with an instructor who gives tips on fun games and ways of introducing your baby safely to the water. You need to negotiate the world of mixed changing rooms, with a baby and possibly a buggy to juggle, but it's worth the hassle.

Take a hike

Taking your baby out for regular walks in the buggy or carrier to a favourite spot helps build a bond and an association with having a good time with Dad. Any parks, fields with horses or cows, pet shops or trains passing can tick a lot of your baby's boxes.

Blow bubbles

You can use bath time bubbles, a cheap bottle of bubbles or else a pot of water with a squirt of washing-up liquid in it and a bit of bent wire (for you, not the baby) to create countless bubbles. Start blowing and watch how they react.

Sofa time

Having your baby lying on your chest isn't just a cutesy photo opportunity; the rhythm of your breathing and the motion of your chest as you inhale and exhale can relax them, and so lead to them associating you with being the go-to guy when a chill-out is needed.

Milestone 14

Baby vomits on you
Age: two weeks–six months

Babies are full of surprises. Sometimes they're so full that bits spill out all over you. They rarely do this when you're dirty, semi-clad and just about to go for a shower. Oh no. Their timing is such that you'll be either in public or at least in your best finery when they launch forth. Their barf is worse than their bite. Baby puke comes in three formats:

1. Posseting – cutesy name for a small amount of sick produced after a feed.
2. Reflux – a bigger puke caused when the still-developing valve at the top of the stomach accidentally opens and the stomach's contents reappear.
3. Projectile vomiting – when your baby brings up his stomach contents in a forceful way. Rare but very alarming. If it happens after every feed, see your doctor.

In general, vomiting is the by-product of mild feeding problems – their tiny tummies can't take all the milk or formula. Occasionally, when it happens in older babies, it's more likely to be caused by an infection, such as gastroenteritis. This type of infection is usually apparent from both ends of your baby. The sick itself isn't that bad. Having to wipe it up is the nauseating bit.

Evasive action
- Wear a muslin when holding, feeding or winding your baby – that's a cloth, which, in theory, your baby pukes on to instead of you. Your baby doesn't know this.
- Feed your baby before they're ravenous – ideally as calmly as possible, too.

- Check their nappy isn't tight on their stomach, that you're only feeding them small amounts and that – if you're using a bottle – the teat or nipple isn't so large that milk or formula pours out easily.

When the puke hits the van ...
Car seat/interior
Scrape off what you can and rinse with warm water. Next, go to work with a citrus-based degreaser/upholstery cleaner. Brush off. Spray with an enzyme cleaner to kill any smelly bacteria. Brush hard several more times, then vacuum to remove the vomit smell.

Carpet/home furnishings
Pick up as much of the vomit as possible, blot the area dry with kitchen paper, then sprinkle with baking soda or cornstarch (note: buy baking soda on day one). The powder absorbs the spew and, when dry, can just be vacuumed up.

Best suit
Never attempt to remove the stain before you get the suit dry-cleaned – you'll just ingrain the puke further. Slip off your jacket, wipe off the 'excess' then sling it over your shoulder and walk straight to the dry-cleaners.

Milestone 15

First decent night's sleep
Age: four–six months, if you're lucky

'Exactly 4 hours and 20 minutes' is the answer to the question 'How much sleep you get on average a night during the baby's first few weeks at home?' in a survey of 3000 new mums and dads.

In all, it's estimated that a new parent loses about 350 hours of sleep over their baby's first year. So, if you've managed to stay awake to the end of that sentence, congrats – you're doing a cracking job already. It can get to a point when some parents don't mind if the noise they hear in the middle of the night *is* a burglar, so long as it's not their kid waking up again.

Two- and three-year-olds still tend to wake up twice a night on average. And that's before they reach school age – at which point exposure to other kids and their germs, plus an aversion to a double period of maths, will give you countless more unsettled nights.

Parenthood is a marathon of sleep deprivation, which, you'll not be surprised to learn, is outlawed as a form of torture. Your baby's role at this time is one of torturer. His or her ability to sleep for the bulk of the day (on average 16 hours' snoozing) but still wake you up at precisely the moment when you are at your most relaxed is down to his or her circadian rhythm or body clock not having set itself properly yet.

Survival guide
To survive, you could try nodding off by counting the number of surveys there are about new parents and their lack of sleep, or adopt a few of the following tactics other dads have used to get some shut-eye:

- Lighten up. Just like jet-lagged adults, the best way to reset a body clock is with the aid of natural light. Getting outside during the day as often as possible will help establish sleep patterns. Some parents are even reverting to the old-school approach of leaving the baby in a pram outside to have a nap (just a nap, not a whole night).

- Go blind. Equally, a blackout blind that plunges the nursery into darkness helps babies begin to establish the pattern of sleeping; newborn babies produce very little of their own darkness hormone, melatonin.
- Stick to the routine. Mealtimes, bath time and bedtime can all create a reassuring habit that makes your baby feel secure and more at ease. Studies show that babies can pick up on bad vibes around the home, too, whereas creating a settling routine and sticking to it can make the nights go more smoothly.
- Be a bore. Night-time feedings are unavoidable but if you can make them as dull as possible – avoiding anything else that can stimulate your baby, like eye contact or talking – they'll settle back to sleep again a whole lot more quickly.
- Don't take to the wheel. Those stories of parents who spend half the night kerb crawling because their baby will only sleep to the motion of the car are based in fact. Kids do fall asleep in cars, though at this stage of new parenthood it could be that the adult drops off first. Where possible, try to settle them without leaving the house.

Milestone 16

Making a splash at bath time

Age: week one

Bath time is a treasured moment for new parents – especially those who spend all day at work and want a bit of bonding time before either baby or parent passes out. It can be a very therapeutic event for both parties; scientists say that the warm, soothing experience of bathing a baby provokes the release of happy hormone oxytocin in many dads. It's also quite daunting and a bit weird at first, though, especially as until the baby's umbilical cord has dropped off you've got an extra dangly bit to deal with. If you have a baby bath specifically for the purpose you may want to use that inside your own big bath – or, at a push, the kitchen sink will do.

First-time tactics are:

- Use a little (12.5cm/5in depth) warm (37°C/98°F) water.
- Have all the gear – cloths, baby shampoo, towel, rubber ducky etc. – nearby. Never leave your nipper alone to 'freestyle' in the bath.
- Lower them in legs first, using your arm to support the neck and head.
- With that one hand supporting them, use the other to gently swish the water over them with the other. If you're using soap, avoid putting it over your baby's face.
- Wash them all over – creases under the chin, genitals, feet.
- Make funny faces and noises to relax your child (hopefully). Even though they spent nine months paddling in an amniotic sac newborns still find baths a bit bemusing on the whole.
- Dab them dry with a towel.
- Apply whatever lotions and potions you have invested in.
- Dress them and put on a fresh nappy, just in time for them to poo or spew again.

Benefits all round

Once you've got it sussed, bath time becomes a key part of the daily routine. Not only are they often in need of a clean-up, but the whole bathing, drying and dressing for bed process also helps them get settled for sleep at night – well, that's the theory at least. If you're working during the day but your partner is at home with the baby, bath time can become a crucial opportunity for fathers to have a bit of hands-on bonding at the end of the day. As your baby grows and starts to find bathing a fun experience these moments become even more beneficial to creating that bond. For this reason, whatever the demands your job may entail, many a dad will tell you that making it home for bath time with your child is well worth the soaking you get.

Milestone 17

Baby finds what you've been hiding

Age: three months onwards

Peek-a-boo games will soon dominate your waking hours as a new father. This opportunity to take on the 'fun dad' persona kicks in a lot earlier than many of us realise. What seems like the dumbest of games is actually quite crucial to cognitive development. Think about it: the fun element of a peek-a-boo and hide-and-seek activity is a bit 'out there'. However, it's not only funny but it also teaches the concept of 'object permanence' – or the idea that things still exist even when you can't see or touch them. To us adults it's all quite obvious (hopefully ...), but to the developing mind of a baby it's the damnedest thing. 'One moment he was there ... Now he's gone ... Oh wait, he's back again!' Hence the laughter, or sometimes tears, as the idea of things vanishing and returning starts to take root.

Why it's worth making an arse of yourself

- Some babies can latch on to the idea of object permanence from as early as three months – and it helps reassure them when you put them to bed, exit the room or leave them strapped in their buggy in the pub's beer garden. It's not until they're around nine months old, however, that they realise that you're still there when your face is covered.
- Your child will probably be fascinated by these disappearing and reappearing acts. Without meaning to sound too woolly, playing these kinds of games will help older babies to develop some simple problem-solving skills as well as to grasp the concept of volume as they begin to take up toddling and trying to hide big things into appropriately sized places (see cat and washing machine).

- Hiding toys encourages exploration and activity – as well as testing a parent's own memory ('Bugger, where did I put Snuggles now? I need him so Gavin can take a nap'). It'll also help you discover great places in which to stash your car keys or wallet once your kid is old enough to seek these out.

Other games

Hide the rattle
As the name suggests, this involves shaking a baby rattle so the infant can see it, then moving it out of his or her eyeline and giving it another shake. This triggers them to start following the sound and moving their head to find out where it's coming from.

Rollerball
No, we don't mean the violent-fighting-on-rollerskates movie, but games with baby-friendly balls – colourful fabric, bells inside – that involve you rolling them to and fro across the floor. Once your baby is able to sit up, these games help them to follow movement with their eyes and develop strength and dexterity to the point where you're able to blame their throwing ability on the breakages you caused when Mum was out of the room.

Milestone 18

Baby gets 'sign language'
Age: six months onwards

Much to-do is made about a baby's first words, as if that's the groundbreaking moment when they start communicating with you. That said (see what I did there), some kids don't utter a word for two years after they're born ... probably through utter disbelief at what they've been born into.

However, even if they don't use words, they will be communicating in that primitive, natural, non-talky way that we've done as animals since the dawn of time. If you're sharp enough you'll pick up on what they're telling you and, even better, find a way of getting a head start on the whole father–child chat thing.

Baby signing

The way to do this is through baby sign language – a concept devised by a child development expert called Dr Joseph Garcia after he had observed how the hearing babies of deaf parents easily copied their parents' signs and used them to communicate. He also spotted how these 'signing' babies were less demanding than non-signing babies because they could express what they wanted and be understood more easily (that's your motivation for learning the following baby signing right there).

From around nine months onwards, babies can start to use a mix of gestures, gurns, gasps and gabs to communicate. Baby signing is a way of refining these, enabling you to make yourself understood to them, and impressing bystanders in the cafe. Much of it resembles 'Makaton', the fairly obvious form of 'signing' that helps kids linguistically develop at nursery. The key thing is to say the word, make the sign and, if possible, include what you're talking about – the bottle of milk – every time at first. Once they get the hang of it they'll make the sign and try to say the word.

A few of the key phrases and witty one-liners to try out on your kid are:

- 'Milk' – fan out hand then clench it like you're milking a cow.
- 'Bath' – run your hands around your torso like you're washing yourself.
- 'More' – pointing your fingertips to your lips (also used for 'food' and 'eat').
- 'All gone' – move your hand, palm up, backwards and forwards.
- 'Baby' – arms crossed, palms up, rocking from side to side.
- 'Butterfly' – crossing hands at the wrists and flapping.

Now see if you can get your baby to sign their milestone first sentence before they can even speak a coherent word ... 'Baby eat butterfly ... All gone!'

Milestone 19

Baby gets to grips with you
Age: four months

As yet no scientific formula has been devised to challenge the curiosity, reflexes and grip strength of a baby as effectively as when you wear jewellery or spectacles within their grasp. Except for ... the palmar grasp reflex test – a technique you can use to check your baby's hand muscle and finger grip development.

The test is performed by simply rubbing the baby's palm with your little finger, at which point, in a Venus fly trap motion, your baby should close its fist and lock tight. The time to play this game is when they're around five months old, although this reflex appears in a baby before it's even born. You'll maybe notice how they squeeze their hand into a tight ball anyway. Once you dab your fingertip into their palm you'll feel that primitive, instinctive grab – said to derive from the time when our ancestors swung from treetops and babies held on for dear life.

Other reflex tests
Along with the palmar grasp reflex test, a few other tests to do with your little monkey include:

- Rooting reflex. Stroke your infant's cheek. It'll turn its head and open its mouth.
- Sucking reflex. Touch the roof of their mouth (wash your hands first) and it'll start to suck your finger.
- Snout reflex. Apply a little light pressure on your little un's closed lips with your finger and they'll start puckering up their lips.
- Galant reflex. This is a newborn reflex that can be seen when you hold your baby face down and stroke along one side of the spine. They should react by flexing their hips with their feet kicking up.

This is one of the checks done at birth to identify any brain or nervous cord issues.

- Moro reflex. This is the name for the times when baby flails its arms to the side, jerks suddenly – even cries out – and startles the hell out of you. The Moro is a built-in survival mechanism designed to protect them – possibly from falling out of trees, the evolution experts suggest. It is one of the reasons why people swaddle their baby, as this reduces the movement and stops the baby from waking itself up when this reflex strikes.
- Babinski sign. Stroking the edges of the sole of the foot from heel to toe makes a baby flex their foot, fan their toes and stretch their big toe.

Aside from being great fun, these reactions are useful indicators that your baby's muscular and nervous systems are developing. A failure to respond to these tests when carried out by experts can alert them to possible conditions such as cerebral palsy.

Twerking and jerking
Babies aren't immune to engaging in some very weird behaviour at times, which can freak out the unsuspecting new parents. Twitching and twerking, hiccupping, head banging, rocking from side to side, staring into space and gripping on to you with a vice-like grasp are all perfectly normal acts among the baby section of the human race as they develop and find out what their bodies can and can't do.

Milestone 20

When you hear yourself speaking in months

Age: from the first trimester of pregnancy until your kid is about three years old ... or 36 months

It kicks in before the birth. Pregnancy is measured in 'trimesters' – three-month stages that tie in with the various weigh-ins and scans to measure growth and development in the lead-up to their EDD – estimated due date.

Once your baby's been born, it's good form to age them by months. They're not a year-and-a-half, they're 18 months old. They're not two, they're 24 months old. This plays havoc with your own adult calendar as you find yourself speaking in months all the time. It's just another of those unseen psychological impacts of parenting creeping into your life.

Other lessons parenting will teach you

Baby ...

- Sticking to the routine. Babies are, like adults, creatures of habit, though it's usually only babies who go into meltdown when that routine is disrupted. Once the daily routine has been established – feed, naps, change, feed, naps, bath, bed – stick to it.
- You only need nappies and a cot. For about the first four to six months these are the essential baby accessories. Everything else is clutter. As lovely as some of those 'baby gifts' and furnishings are – the knitted bonnet, clothes hamper, mini Adidas retro sneakers – in reality, babies just eat, poo and sleep.
- You need to treasure every moment. Yes, it's a soppy thing to say but these early weeks, months and years will fly by. Even though it may feel like an eternity when they won't sleep or are going through the agonies of teething, pretty soon you'll be looking at pictures of them as a baby or flogging clothes from the newborn stage and find yourself getting all sentimental over how tiny they were.
- Anything goes. In their mouths if you're not watching them. When they've developed the ability to do so, your baby will just love to put anything and everything into their mouth.

Toddler ...

- Distraction is vital. The moment they fall over, point at the dog being walked down the street, the swings in the park, the ice-cream van. Anything that distracts from their fall and breaks their instinct to bawl at double-figure decibels. Make a fuss and they'll play the role of victim full blare.
- Bed is a good place to go. Never make the bed or the bedroom a punishment zone or bad place to be. Naughty step, fine, but the bedroom should always be a place they *want* to go to – ideally before the football starts on TV.

Milestone 21

First night out together without your baby
Age: four–six weeks or more

Dust plays a big role in the lives of new parents, in no small part due to the fact that there's a lot of it about soon after baby arrives thanks to you decorating the nursery, unpacking new accessories and not having the energy to do any housework. In time, however, the dust settles and the desire to get back out and enjoy the social interaction that brought you together returns. How long after the birth of your baby you decide to have a night out without them is up to you ... and a legion of internet mums if the forums are anything to go by.

Generally, the time is right when you and the mother both feel comfortable with the thought of leaving baby with a sitter for a few hours. To make that first night out enjoyable without spending three hours FaceTiming your babysitter from the pub closest to your house, follow these steps to success ...

Screen the babysitter
If you haven't entrusted your offspring with a family member or tried-and-trusted sitter then you'll need to carry out your first babysitter interrogation (see Milestone 48). Do book a babysitter and a venue to go to – get tickets too – since the more committed you are to this first post-birth date night the more likely it is to happen.

Settle them in
Avoid having the babysitter arrive five minutes before your taxi does. Baby and sitter need time to settle before parents leave the house. And parents need at least an hour to repeatedly brief the babysitter about food preferences, favourite toy, when to put them to sleep, which phone number to call 'in the event of an emergency', etc.

Say goodbye

Possibly for the first time since they were born, you're going to say farewell to your baby. (OK, it's only a few hours but this is something of a landmark). Saying goodbye lets them know that they can rely on you to let them know what's going on – and if they're only six months old and don't have a clue what that means, at least it gets you into the habit. (They soon also get used to not worrying when you two disappear.) Keep it cheerful and, once the door shuts, either run or speak loudly to your partner to drown out any cries that could jeopardise the whole evening.

Of course, one or both of you will spend most of the evening wondering or worrying about your baby. Any text message or call will send you into a panic and neither of you will achieve the relaxed state of ease and enjoyment that you lie to your babysitter about when you get home. But in the long run, you can show your kids that adult life can be fun and isn't all about doting on your dependents.

Milestone 22

Having a conversation that isn't about your baby

Age: four weeks

Some relationship specialists recommend that parents 'lock the bedroom door' to keep their marriage childproof – in other words using events like date night to rekindle their child-free days and restore the intimacy of their relationship. You could also consider the following the next time you're out together and desperate not to talk about the kids:

1. Don't speak to one another.
2. Go to the cinema (or library or a monastery) where any speaking is a no-no.
3. Spend the night out with a couple of childless friends – you'll still talk about the baby but they will make a decent effort to get you off the topic at every turn.
4. Take flash cards with different topics written on them (e.g. politics, sport, global warming). Bring these into play whenever you feel the conversation drifting off towards such scintillating subjects as school choices, catchment areas or the latest episode of *Thomas & Friends*.
5. Rule: down three fingers' worth of beer, wine or spirits whenever the word 'weaning' or 'nappy' or 'who do you think our baby looks most like?' becomes a topic of conversation.

6. Be envious. This works when they're a bit older. Plan for your kid's night in to be so great – they're having pizza, ice cream, watching a film – that you're almost pissed off at missing out on what they're doing. They then become the unmentioned elephant in the room.
7. Aversion therapy. Go out with the only people who share as close an interest in being new parents and your baby as you do – so your kid's grandparents, or the couple you met at antenatal class or adults with kids the same age as yours. Accept that the baby will be the hot topic and burn on through. Do all the things new parents do when they're out again together for the first time in months or possibly years – eat a meal in five minutes, clear away the table even though you're in a restaurant and coo at other people's babies. Hopefully by the next time you go out you'll have exhausted every angle.

Milestone 23

Baby starts to talk ... almost

Age: any time from six months

Babbling is what they call a baby's first attempts to talk. Most dads have been doing it for years so will recognise this stream of incoherent whoops, yips and coos that were probably once deemed the work of the Devil. These days, it just prompts parents into marvelling at how cute and verbally advanced their baby is, or worrying that he or she is slow on the uptake, or even French. Here's how your kid's speech development should probably take shape ...

Two-three months

This is when a baby's cry starts to sound different – it's more nuanced in different situations – at least according to experts who've managed to put up with the wailing for long enough to differentiate it.

Four-five months

Starts babbling. Literally, that's what it sounds like. They do it a lot, especially when happy. And they might start making consonant sounds like 'ma' and 'da'.

Five-six months

Mimics intonation. Your baby will make their voice rise and fall – it still won't make any sense, but it almost sounds like they're responding to what you're saying while taking on a bit of an Australian accent. 'Ma' and 'da' may become 'mama' and 'dada'.

Seven-12 months

More piss-taking. This time they *will* try to imitate your speech; it almost sounds like they're being sarcastic. (They'll perfect this skill when they're around 14.)

First word!

By the time your baby reaches his or her first birthday you should start hearing words that finally make sense. They may start adding more in a few weeks – or saying nothing else for months. To help encourage their speech try these tips:

1. Chat to them. Speak to them in a simple, clear manner, and often. Don't fret about using 'baby talk' – just chat to them when bathing, feeding or changing a nappy (if you can bear to open your airways).
2. Buddy up. Sit your baby with someone else's baby (this is not a contest) to see how they start babbling or try to out-squeal each other. They may appear to be talking ... about you.
3. Read picture books. Describe what you are looking at to your baby and make sounds, such as 'moo' and 'quack' (where required). From six months, your baby should start to engage with this, usually with a giggle or else a withering look of contempt.

16 months

Toddlers start directing what they're saying towards others. They start adding inflection – words going up in pitch when asking questions. (That Australian accent again.)

18 months

Their vocabulary will be around 10–20 words and by 24 months they'll be using two-word phrases – such as 'Daddy beer'.

If your child isn't talking at all by around 16 months it's worth talking to your GP or postnatal carer. Children develop at different speeds and some need more of a prompt than others ... though you may soon regret getting them started.

Milestone 24

Having sex again
Age: any time from four weeks onwards

It's not so much a developmental landmark as a reminder of what got you to this point in the first place. Many expectant couples fear that sex will become a thing of the past once they become parents; that the baby will come between them and their ability to get physical again.

Certainly, the trauma of birth, the recovery process for Mum and the fact that you're both far too shagged out by night feeds and the change in lifestyle to be nearly as energetic as you were before can all mean that sex does get put on hold for a time once the baby comes along. However, for the majority of parents – obviously those with more than one child – the sex factor does return to relationships. When you do look to get jiggy again, as it were, you should be prepared for the following.

It won't feel the same at first
For a variety of reasons, both partners may find the resumption of activities in the bedroom dept a bit weird and not just because you're out of practice. Hormone levels, muscle tissue relaxation, scarring, tearing and tender boobs from breastfeeding are among the causes of discomfort for the woman at first.

It won't be a priority
The bed becomes the focal point for making up the lack of sleep, which in turn suppresses the libido – anthropologists will tell you that this is nature's way of stopping Mum getting pregnant again too soon (which is, biologically, quite viable within just hours of your child being born).

It can require a slow start

Don't be surprised if one of you really takes a while to feel up to getting intimate again – and don't push too hard to make it happen. The experts suggest a little light kissing or touching at first to at least maintain some intimacy.

It can require a 'quickie'

Foreplay may well be forgotten for the time being as grabbing the opportunity takes precedence – finding a moment when baby's napping, regardless of the time of day, shows ingenuity, as does thinking outside the bed. The bathroom, the walk-in wardrobe or hallway can acquire a whole new attraction at this point. On the flip side, foreplay is probably even more important for a woman recovering from giving birth, so use some lube.

Milestone 25

Baby teeth
Age: six months onwards

At about the time you've finally got your baby settled into a routine that's enabling you all to get some sleep – around six months – their teeth start growing out through their gums. Cue more tears and sleepless nights. There's no hard-and-fast time scale for how long it'll take your baby's teeth to start appearing in their smile, but here's a rough guide to which tooth is probably the culprit according to their age. ...

Which gnashers appear when

Age	Tooth
6–8 months	Front incisors (lower may appear first)
8–10 months	Second (lateral) incisors
12–16 months	First molars (back teeth)
18–22 months	Canines (eye teeth)
24–36 months	Second molars
>36 months	Full set of 20 baby or 'milk' teeth

Chews – your weapons

Typical teething symptoms include inflamed gums, dribbling, ruddy red cheeks, a desire to chew whatever they can get their little hands on, and a drop in appetite. To help ease the discomfort you can try a few teething tricks for tots that reduce some of the pain the parents are feeling too:

- Teething toys. Things such as chewing rings, made from plastic but filled with a cold gel, help to soothe the pain. Pop them in the fridge to chill (not the freezer!), then hand them to your inflamed infant.
- Must-have rusks. An organic alternative to teething rings, these snacks are made from milk and wheat and are designed so that your baby can bite hard without cracking it. Beware: when combined with saliva, the rusks soften to make a revolting mush that babies like to wipe all over themselves, the cat and the furniture, where it sets solid in a few minutes.
- Make a mesh. These are colourful little nets that you fill with fruit (such as pineapple and blueberries) and vegetables, and snap shut. Your baby checks the mesh, sucks out the juice and gets a therapeutic chew going without swallowing any big bits.

Among other ploys adopted by parents hoping to ease the teething pains are amber necklaces, which some people believe release tiny amounts of succinic acid into the baby's bloodstream, helping with pain and drooling; cold strips of cucumber; over-the-counter pain-relief gels (specific to babies); bagels; and pure vanilla extract rubbed on to their gums (this contains alcohol, so, like the gels, numbs the gum temporarily).

Milestone 26

Baby pressures on marital relationship
Age: one month onwards

The whole new life-changing experience that is becoming parents can put a strain on your relationship. Some of the key ingredients for a massive row – fatigue, envy, sex and money or the lack of both the latter – get exacerbated when there's another mouth to feed, sleepless nights, a greater workload for both partners, feelings of isolation and a lack of intimacy. According to one study, arguments among couples increase by 40 per cent in the first year of parenthood – many of which are linked to stress and exhaustion – with topics such as 'whose turn it is to change nappies' and 'who is doing the night feeds' featuring highly. One in five parents polled also said they didn't receive enough attention from their partner after the birth of their baby. Thankfully, there are a few strategies you can use to cope with some of the new challenges becoming a dad will throw into your relationship.

Sticking to the routine
Your baby's sleep and feeding routine will dominate the first few weeks and months of the baby's and your lives. Working around their needs – sacrificing your own time, changing shift patterns, sharing the workload – will lessen the impact this upheaval has on your relationship, but you need to agree with your partner on how you're going to divide up the chores.

Not sweating the small stuff
House-proud parents or obsessive-compulsive types may want to look away now. Even when you do make a greater effort to do more housework there is always going to be a mess when a new baby and all their accessories, or a growing toddler and all their toys, or both, are

on the scene. Agree to accept that this will be the case – at least until they're old enough to earn pocket money for household chores.

Give each other time out

While some of those pre-baby hobbies, such as the four-hour cycle sportive each Saturday morning, may need to be put on hold, parents shouldn't give up all their 'me time' when the baby arrives. Taking a break to indulge in something away from the family – even if it's just for an hour – is vital to keeping you both happy and refreshed.

Hit the sack

Work out a plan, such as taking turns to get up in the middle of the night for baby feeds or doing set nights when one of you covers the whole night. Sleep becomes a precious commodity that both of you will need and be deprived of. Sex may be similarly in short supply, but it's vital that you keep your relationship as strong and intimate as before even if it doesn't involve intercourse. Intimate massages, cuddles, kissing and touching will help keep you close until sex is back on the agenda.

Milestone 27

Baby responds to its own name
Age: around seven months

Here's a test of how fruitful those trials and tribulations over what to call your child were. Will they quickly develop a knack for recognising and responding to the moniker you've bestowed upon them?

When do they respond directly to you calling out their name?

In the womb?	One kick for yes
A few weeks old	That's because they just recognise your voice
5–7 months	They start matching sounds with objects and people
10–12 months	Parroting words you say – including their name!

A handy way of making a name stick – or helping them to learn it a bit quicker – is to use it whenever you talk to your baby. This seems quite obvious. Actually it *is* obvious, but don't be fooled into thinking that just because you chat to your baby they'll pick up this whole lingo lark naturally. They will learn it through repetition.

A lot of store is set by speech development in babies and toddlers because it's not easy learning to speak from scratch and kids do it at different stages. Also, children with significant social delays, such as those with autism spectrum disorder (ASD), often don't respond to their name when called. Just to confuse matters more, children without autism can also have difficulty with this.

Rough guidelines to how a baby should progress

By 12 months old they can:

- Respond to their name most of the time when you call it.
- Wave goodbye.
- Babble with intonation (as if they're speaking in sentences).
- Say anything from 'Da-da' to 'Dad!!!!'

By 18 months old they can:

- Follow simple instructions when you speak and gesture.
- Point to their head, toes, belly, etc. when you ask them to.
- Learn one new word per week.

Not every child will follow this path exactly and regular health checks can often pick up on developmental setbacks.

As an aside, don't be alarmed by the size or behaviour of babies who are a similar age to your own, and beware the exaggerated claims of some parents about their own kid's development ('Petronella was playing the piano at five months'). All this can panic you into thinking that your child isn't growing the way they should be for their age. Children go through spurts in their development – often growing by about 30cm (12in) in one go the day after you've just bought a lorry load of Babygros.

If you are concerned that your child's development is a little on the slow side or if you're worried about their speech – or lack of it – it's certainly worth telling your doctor. They're most likely to reassure you by repeating something similar to the last couple of sentences you've just read, but they may also want to investigate a little further.

Milestone 28

First photos of your baby
Age: day one onwards

It's easy to dismiss the 'art' of photographing a wriggling baby in an age of smartphones that means you can take as many photos as you want, but for pictures you want to share – or your partner will allow you to share when she's just been through 25 hours of labour – there are a few things you can do.

Note: if it really is the first pic of the baby, taken just after their delivery, then don't go for the natural – post-birth blood and awe – pic unless it's for your own private collection. Instead, let Mum have a moment to get ready for a photo, or else let her refuse to be in it.

Find the best light

Not ideal on a labour ward or in the delivery suite ... They're not places known for their serenity and natural lighting. Neither Mum nor your baby will be that impressed with a flash going off in their face, so see if you can reposition a lamp or open the blinds before taking it. 'Aim to have the children in brightly lit areas – like outside or in window-lit areas in the day,' suggests photographer Rowan Letlow. 'Images that are intended to be put on social media do not necessarily need to have the most dynamic and contrasted lighting. It's all about the story of the image.'

Check before you send

Are your baby's features clear enough for people to see them when you share the photo? This needs to be so in order to elicit an 'Ooo, she's got her dad's nose' response. Is Mum OK with how she's looking in this captured moment? Are there any wires, bloody clothes, bits of umbilical cord, nipples or other private parts in shot that you may want to cut out?

First family pics

If you're looking to take some quality images of your baby once they're home follow some pro photographer rules, namely: try to shoot any pics of your baby during the 'magic hour' – usually the first hour after sunrise. This is when natural light is at its most radiant – and it's when you'll probably be awake for the first six months anyway.

'Don't underestimate the power of an image captured at night though,' says Letlow. 'Perhaps when your child is reading/being read a bedtime story or brushing their teeth. I find the most powerful and fun pictures come from those that are not posed, but fleeting moments that are captured at the right time.'

❛ Dad tales: Enlarge them!

We took regular, monthly pics of our baby in the same spot – beside her teddy bear – which was like a sense of scale. It made a nice record of how she was growing. ❜

Paul, dad of Tom and Layla

Make the model happy

Kids of any age don't hide discomfort well. If they won't co-operate for your family portrait or happy snap then check for possible reasons, such as a wet nappy, their clothes being too tight, them being hungry – the kind of thing that makes us adults grouchy, too. Failing that, a favourite toy waved just out of shot can elicit a bigger smile than enforced time with the rest of the family ever will.

'Sometimes children do not like to be photographed, or when they do the picture can look stiff and dull,' warns Letlow. 'Incorporating some form of entertainment for them can hugely enhance the story and life of the image, be it a bottle, teddy bear, or even another person to interact with.'

Go for coloured clothing

'It's a safe bet to go with the baby blue and pink colours. To be honest, any bright and vibrant colours will work great. Yellow tops on a sunny day and white dresses in a park are great,' says Letlow.

If all else fails then a free download of Adobe Photoshop Express and some creative work with the settings should crop out the mess and even put a fake smile on your little one's chops.

Milestone 29

Transition to solids
Age: around four months

> 'Alexa ... Feed my kids.'
>
> Dadsnet

If your baby's mother has managed to persist with breastfeeding for the best part of the first six months, then the 'weaning' process is the time when you can get more involved in the nourishment side of things. Weaning is the name for the time when babies shift from mainly liquid to mainly solid food. 'Solid' here is a loose term. Much of the mush they eat at around this time (between four and six months onwards) is little more than puréed fruit, jars of paste-like vegetable mixtures, and baby rice porridge. Despite appearances, this is perfect for this stage in the development of the baby's digestive system and it takes some of the pressure off Mum's boobs or the baby formula and bottle washer.

Baby buffet
As your baby grows into the weaning phase you might want to look at your seating arrangements. If they're sitting up OK and holding their head to feed then a highchair may come in handy at mealtimes.

First, you need to go through the logistics and get a highchair that's:

- safe and secure – make sure there's a safety restraint
- adult friendly – you can put it together
- cleanable – with removable or wipe-down tray and covers.

You can then look at your weaning options.

Spoon-fed – You feed smooth mashed food to your baby, progressing to thicker foods containing soft lumps and then on to minced and chopped food from around nine months.

Baby-led – You offer them 'finger foods', so they eat what they like and you're left with what they don't. It's messier, but it can help in their checking, tasting and dexterity development. Here are some finger food ideas:

- sticks of cucumber (see also teething in Milestone 25)
- sticks of Cheddar cheese
- carrot sticks (there is a 'sticks' theme here)
- banana, broken into chunks
- rice cakes.

Weaning on to solids doesn't just happen overnight. For a while, you and your partner may find mealtimes for your baby taking on a more 'fusion'-focused style – bottle or breast, purées and/or solids according to how your baby is adapting to the transition and what the pair of you can be bothered to do at mealtimes. Be patient and prepare for some hiccups – both literally and metaphorically – as your baby progresses through the weaning stage.

Milestone 30

First steps
Age: nine months onwards ... and onwards

It's up there with his or her 'first word' in the developmental landmark stages of early years. The time your child takes their first steps – walking without support – is a 'don't miss it' moment. To reduce the odds of you not being there to witness that first great step, here's what the build-up looks like ...

Crawl
What? They finally manage to raise themselves up on their hands and knees and shuffle across the floor. Usually preceded by some rocking backwards and forwards before they manage to move forwards, or backwards (they often crawl backwards first).
When? Around six months old.
Dad's role? Get down on hands and knees to see what life looks like for a six-month-old kid.

On the pull
What? Having developed leg and arm strength, they're now pulling themselves up on the bars of their cot, the stair gate, the tablecloth.
When? Around 10 months
Dad's role? Remove tablecloth.

Cruising
What? How a soon-to-be toddler makes their way around the room using whatever furniture is available.
When? 10–12 months.
Dad's role? Make furniture available.

Walking

What? One morning they'll get the balls to go up on two legs and joyfully stumble towards the sofa (think drunk's sense of direction and co-ordination but on a smaller scale).

When? Any time between 9 and 16 months.

Dad's role? Your work has only just begun. Baby push-along toys or 'toddle trucks' encourage them to get more stable on their feet – if it's a push-along vacuum cleaner, even better!

Top toddling tips

- Where possible, make sure your baby has a soft landing and fit stair gates at the top and bottom of the stairs once they start taking an interest in crawling up them.
- Hold off fitting those cool mini Adidas trainers or indeed any shoes until your baby is walking around outside or on cold surfaces regularly. Going barefoot will help them develop their balance and coordination.
- By about the age of 36 months your baby should be walking up and down stairs – one step at a time – as well as running, jumping and standing freely. They may still need to think harder about things like standing on tiptoe and still find it a challenge to balance while on one foot, too.

Milestone 31

Taking baby to a pub
Age: six months

'Dogs welcome, children must be kept on a lead.'

Pub sign

For some, it's a landmark moment in the introduction of a new baby to the local community. For others, it's the topic of endless online parenting forum debate. Pub-going parents may see taking your baby to the local as a bit of a rite of passage. It could be a one-off 'meet the regulars' and wet the baby's head (not literally) visit, a family get-together at a gastropub that allows babies (always phone and check), or it could be that your regular Sunday afternoon stroll always seems to take in the boozer showing the live match.

Whatever the excuse for the excursion, take note of this cobbled-together 'code of conduct' – accrued from dads who've bravely gone before so that you can follow – to ensure it's an enjoyable visit for everyone involved.

Time, gentlemen
If your baby hasn't yet settled into a routine, or if he has but you're hoping to visit the pub when they're most likely to need a feed or a change, or both, then maybe think again. An unsettled baby will just lead to unsettled pub regulars. Show a bit of consideration for others and if your baby does kick off, abandon your visit.

Just a swift one
Don't make plans to settle in for the whole afternoon – unless you're keen on meeting up with social services. Even for a short trip, take a change of nappy (and hope there's a place in the pub where you can do the change – definitely not on the bar) and a feed or snack.

Pick your spot

A family-friendly pub or a quiet area in a local you know is a good option. Pitching the buggy beside the dance floor and karaoke machine on a Saturday night, not so much. If you're off for a family meal, check that the pub has highchairs and a kid's menu when booking a table.

Keep them busy

If your child is toddling then opt for somewhere that has an outdoor play area. Pubs are dangerous places for kids to be running around in thanks to a mixture of hard furniture, glass fragments and intoxicated adults. If you're sitting indoors, take a bag of toys or colouring equipment (nothing that makes a noise) or books to keep them occupied. ('Books' is just me being aspirational – iPads and tablets have long since usurped these as many parents' digital distraction of choice, but at least I tried.)

Milestone 32

Moments of panic
Age: week one onwards

All new parents experience at least one breakout bout of anxiety about their child's development early in the little one's life. Just as adults can look on the internet to identify a blister they've found on their foot and within moments have self-diagnosed buboes last seen during the Black Death, so many of us draw alarming conclusions about our infant's health and well-being based on a bit of odd behaviour.

This panic can strike within moments of them being born and be triggered by some pretty natural – but unexpected – side effects to having just popped out a womb.

Alarming things babies do but are nothing to worry about

- Startle reflex – also called the 'Moro reflex'. Your baby will spontaneously splay out its arms – jazz hands style – and even let out a loud gasp. They're experiencing what can be best described as a sensation of free falling. They grow out of this after about six months.
- Irregular breathing. They suddenly start holding their breath for what seems like ages (up to 10 seconds in some cases). They especially love doing this when you're listening to them on the bedroom baby monitor. It's known as periodic breathing. It's quite normal – almost like they're winding you up.
- Going scaly. Babies can develop what's called 'cradle cap' – which is as normal as it is greasy, yellow and rash-like.

And on the other hand...

Some behaviours to be wary of, or seek medical advice about, if you notice they persist:

- not smiling back at you when you do
- not noticing when you enter or leave the room
- having difficulty responding to some noises
- not wanting to cuddle or not responding to cuddling.

The importance of regular checks

Sometimes, delays in development can be an indication of anything from hearing loss to autism spectrum disorder (ASD). Attending regular postnatal check-ups and seeking advice from medical professionals as your baby grows will usually help identify any issues or allay any fears.

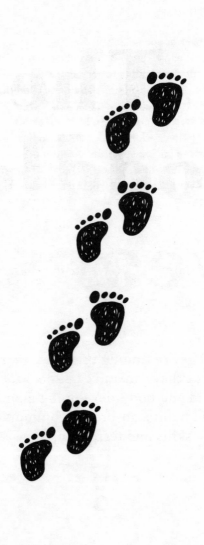

The toddler years...

They're finding their feet, learning what they can and can't do, growing in mind and body, developing mannerisms and habits, absorbing communication skills and terrorising the cat ...

Milestone 33

Path to potty training
Age: 24 months onwards

From around 18 months onwards another 'transition' can begin. This time the solids are already involved. It's potty training time. Keep in mind that the key word in potty training is 'training'. There is no one-potty-fits-all solution, but dads can play a major role in helping their child adapt to this – often by coming up with their own novel prompts or techniques to encourage their baby to take a seat.

To get you started, here are some tried-and-tested tips from dads who've boldly gone before...

Drop hints

At first, your kid will just forget that they need to switch from going in their nappy to now going to the potty. Asking them if they need to go to the potty will help get them into the mindset. They may just do as you ask and sit on the potty because they don't want to have an accident, but then just sit there drawing a blank. It'll take some persistence on both the child's and the parents' parts for them to get the timing right and come up with the goods.

Bogside reading

Get them into a happy habit when using the potty, perhaps by giving them a book they can look at while they go. There are books for potty training children to read that feature potty training. Yep, it's that big a deal getting them into 'the zone'. Talking about their favourite toy or doll using the potty and even customising their potty or the space around it to make it a fun little retreat can help it become a habit.

Keep calm and carry on

Try not to cause your kid any unnecessary stress or anxiety around their toilet habits. It'll take time for them to get the confidence and competence needed to go to the potty. In time, you'll also be looking to train them to use the toilet – possibly with a toddler-size seat fitted and a stool.

In loo of reward

A daily tick chart beside the potty – celebrating each successful trip – or a treat when they go a whole day without needing their nappy can be good ways of encouraging them to become more independent when it comes to toilet training. Avoid telling them off when they don't get to the potty in time or making them fearful because of toilet mishaps – you could literally make them crap themselves and so compound things further. Instead, incentivise them with praise and offer a 'high five' ... then wash your hands.

Potty training can be a challenge and pretty messy at first. But if your morning ritual has already involved nappy changing, disposing of dirty diapers and even wiping Sudocrem down an arse crack that's not your own then you'll be prepared for what's about to come.

Milestone 34

Time for baby number two?
Age: 20 months onwards

It's not unusual for couples to fall pregnant again within a year of the birth of their first baby, through choice or accident, though the average gap between siblings in the UK is around three years and eight months. For some parents, the plus points to having a smaller age gap go beyond the youngest child receiving still-fashionable cast-off clothes from their older brother or sister.

If you're having the conversation with a view to imminent fertilisation then draw a couple of columns on the back of your longest supermarket receipt – there'll be plenty of those around the house – and consider some of the following ...

Pros
- Clothes will still be in vogue for the younger brother or sister!
- You've got a taste for bringing up a baby.
- Child 1 will have a like-minded playmate who's close in years.
- They can share a bedroom for a few years before you need to think about finding a bigger home.
- Child 2 will get a priority school place if Child 1 is already attending the school.

Cons
- Talk to your GP about timing. (A gap of less than 17 months between babies has been linked with an increased risk of premature or underweight babies.)

- Consider how you are both managing with Child 1 and ask yourselves what impact the sleep routine and going back to work has had upon you both.
- Work out whether you can afford another child, especially now that you've seen what it costs having another mouth to feed.

Age matters

A couple of key issues to discuss when it comes to having more children, especially later in life, are to do with the impact that age can have on a successful pregnancy. Although 66 per cent of women aged 35 will conceive naturally and have a baby within a year of trying, after this age it can become more difficult to fall pregnant – and statistically the chance of miscarriage rises, too.

It's not just about the mother's age, either. The older 'dad' is the longer it may take you to get your partner pregnant. It's estimated that the chances of conception taking more than a year are around 8 per cent when you're under 25 – but by the time you're 35 that figure doubles. The risk of miscarriage is twice as high if the father is over 45 – and that's completely independent of the age of the mother.

Fit to father more kids?

Age: from when your first child is one

While some feckless types and prominent politicians seem to be able to sire offspring at the drop of their trousers, research shows that 35–40 per cent of the fertility complications couples experience are down to male infertility problems. Because of men's general reluctance to ask for help in matters health-related, many men remain uninformed about the potential fertility issues they may come up against when they want to start a family or have more children. Below are a few factors to consider when you're trying for another child.

Infertility has many causes

About 90 per cent of male infertility cases are due to low sperm count or poor sperm quality – this can be caused by a number of reasons, including varicocele (an abnormal collection of bulging veins above the testicle), infections, genetic abnormalities and hormone problems. Slow sperm motility, which makes it harder for sperm to swim to the egg, and odd-shaped sperm are other common causes.

Keeping your balls cool will help

According to experts, such as fertility specialists at the IVI Group, sperm requires a very precise environment in which to live healthily – and that's 4°C (39.2°F) cooler than the rest of the body (hence why your testicles hang around outside the body). Excessive heat can warp sperm, so experts insist you don't rest your computer on your lap, don't spend too long in the sauna but where possible, wear loose boxer shorts instead of tight briefs.

Avoid stress

Stress can affect sperm count by lowering levels of a hormone called gonadotrophin-releasing hormone (GnRH) (see Milestone 74), which is needed for sperm production. Trying some relaxation techniques, or even chilling out to yoga, may help to ease the strain when you're trying for a baby. Alcohol is also toxic to the testes and the IVI experts suggest that drinking more than 20 units per week can affect your chances of conceiving.

Fit for life

Keeping physically and mentally fit for fatherhood can ensure that you're able to have children later in life, too, because it can ease stress and help maintain good-quality sperm. Also, eating foods that are rich in antioxidants, such as tomatoes, blueberries, and pomegranates, is said to provide an added boost when trying for a baby.

Milestone 36

Doctor Dad – at-a-glance guide to child illnesses
Age: six months onwards

As far back as the prenatal scans and checks, parents get a crash course in concerns about their baby's health and well-being – preparing you and your vocabulary for the likes of jaundice, colic, cradle cap, croup, colds, constipation and nappy rash. While these sound like the names of seven sickly dwarfs, they are just some of the ailments youngsters can succumb to seemingly within minutes of them being born.

In fact, these illnesses help your little one to build their immunity and prepare them for another round of germ warfare when they enter nursery. They also prepare first-time parents for some of the ups and downs ahead. Consulting your child's GP or calling NHS Direct is obviously the best route to go down whenever you're concerned about their health, but it's worth knowing a few of the possible causes, symptoms and advice you'll be given when your kid gets sick.

Childhood illnesses and what to expect

Illness	Symptoms	Treatment	Advice
Chicken pox	Rash of red flat spots that develop into itchy blisters	Chemist	Back to nursery/ school 5 days after onset of rash
Common cold	Runny nose, sneezing, sore throat, headache	Chemist	Wash hands frequently

Illness	Symptoms	Treatment	Advice
Conjunctivitis	Teary, red, itchy, painful eye(s)	Chemist	Try not to touch eyes; notify nursery/school
Flu	Fever, coughs, sneezes, headache, body aches, exhaustion, sore throat	GP	Ask GP to confirm as symptoms may not be due to flu
Glandular fever	High temperature, sore throat, swollen glands	GP	Child needs to be physically able to concentrate; notify nursery/school
Hand, foot and mouth disease	Fever, sore throat, headache, blisters inside the mouth and on hands and feet	GP	Off nursery/school until recovered; notify nursery/school
Head lice	Itchy scalp	Chemist	Shampoo treatment, notify nursery/school
Impetigo	Clusters of red bumps or blisters surrounded by area of redness	GP	Back to nursery/school when lesions crust or 48 hours after start of antibiotics; notify nursery/school
Measles	Fever, cough, runny nose watery inflamed eyes; small red spots with white or bluish-white centres in the mouth, red, blotchy rash	GP	Back to nursery school 4 days from onset of rash; notify nursery/school

Illness	Symptoms	Treatment	Advice
Ringworm	Red ring-shaped rash, may be itchy; rash may be dry, scaly, wet or crusty	GP	Go with GP's advice; notify nursery/school
Rubella	Fever, tiredness, red rash that starts on the face and spreads downwards	GP	Back to nursery/school 6 days from onset of rash; notify nursery/school
Scabies	Intense itching, pimple-like rash between the fingers, wrists and elbows	GP	Back to nursery/school after first treatment; notify nursery/school
Shingles	Pain, itching or tingling along the affected nerve pathway; blister-type rash	GP	Stay off nursery/school if rash is weeping and can't be covered; notify nursery/school
Sickness bug	Stomach cramps, nausea, vomiting and diarrhoea	Chemist	See GP if symptoms persist after 48 hours; notify nursery/school
Threadworms	Intense itchiness around anus	Chemist	Ensure good hand hygiene; notify nursery/school
Tonsilitis	Intense sore throat, temperature, trouble swallowing	GP	Medication, fluids, off nursery/school until fully recovered

Illness	Symptoms	Treatment	Advice
Whooping cough	Violent coughing, over and over until child inhales with 'whoop' sound to get air into lungs	GP	Back to nursery/school 48 hours after starting antibiotics or three weeks after coughing first started; notify nursery/school

(See www.patient.co.uk if you want more expert advice on this)

‘ Dad tales

With respect to illnesses, it's not too bad from birth to pre-school bar the inevitable few doctors visits, but after that it's constant sickness of one sort or another. ❞

Chris Smith, father of Millie, Molly and Nellie

Milestone 37

Writing a will – who should raise your kids if you die?

Age: one day

Becoming a father opens up a whole new world of conversations you never thought you'd find yourself having. The responsibility that comes with the transition from lad to dad and the realisation that you now have dependants can also lead to you having to consider what if, God forbid, you both cash in your chips well before your time?

In a bid to cater for the needs of their children, many new parents will write a will and appoint guardians to cover this unthinkable – but not unknown – situation. It all gets a bit serious at this point, but for peace of mind it's worth doing. If you fail to appoint guardians in your will and your children are orphaned before they reach 18, the courts will appoint guardians instead, but they won't necessarily choose the people who you would have preferred to take care of your children. By appointing guardians you can ensure that your kids are looked after by the people you'd most like to do the job.

Choose wisely

This can be a reason to update your will regularly, too. If the guardian you choose lives nearby it'll help give your kids some stability at a time of major upset, as they won't need to change schools, leave friends, etc. The ages of close relatives and grandparents should be also considered when updating the will.

Check that they want to raise your kids

If your brother says 'Yes, of course I'll bring my nephew up … What's his name again?' take this as a clue that he's just acquiescing to please you. The appointed person also needs to think about what it could entail before agreeing to be a guardian.

Cover your assets

You may trust your guardian with your kids, but that doesn't mean you have to trust them with your cash. Any assets you have can be put into trust so that your kid gets access to them at a certain age, or can be overseen – as per your instructions – by a trustee.

Document a plan

Put everything in writing. Not just who you want to be guardians, and why, but also who you don't want to do the job. Be explicit about your reasons – any offence you cause by not wanting shady Uncle Jack to look after the kids won't be a worry for you by the time your justification comes out.

The Citizens Advice service provides details about how to create a legal, binding will. You can also buy them off the shelf in stationery stores or download a template document to fill in and file with a solicitor or trustee.

Milestone 38

First-time first aid
Age: week one

You'd think that a small child who's barely able to do more than eat, drink, poo and sleep can't really come to any major harm. That's until you see the list of possibilities first aid courses can train you to deal with: choking, croup, febrile convulsion (I looked it up: seizures), dislocations, severe allergic reactions, foreign object in nose or ear, unresponsive and not breathing, unresponsive and breathing, asthma attack, dehydration, meningitis and nose bleeds. According to the Royal Society for the Prevention of Accidents (RoSPA) those most at risk from a home accident are the zero–four years age group.

God forbid you have to go through the experience of having to administer first aid to your infant, but being prepared for it could literally make you a lifesaver. Parents can take first aid classes especially for babies before or after their kids arrive – in the UK they're run by the St John Ambulance and Red Cross, and will give you some confidence and competence.

Get tooled up
A family first aid kit should probably be the first thing you buy as a new dad – though not as the 'birth gift' for the new mum. It'll be useful for the less traumatic traumas your child puts you through and should feature bandages, swabs, antiseptic spray or wipes, thermometer and a first aid booklet.

Choke action
If your baby starts choking on something lodged in its throat hold them face down along your thigh with their head lower than their bum. Hit them firmly on their back between the shoulder blades up to

five times. These back blows will create a vibration and pressure in the airway, which is often enough to dislodge the blockage – ensure you support their head while you hold them in position.

Baby CPR

In the event of your infant being unresponsive and not breathing then the first move is to call an ambulance. If you can begin CPR then do. The basic moves are to check their airway is clear and open – sweeping a finger through the front of the mouth to clear it if necessary – then turn your baby into the recovery position on their side and, if they're still not breathing, perform CPR with your fingertips, puffing small breaths into their mouth and nose with your own mouth to try to resuscitate them. The first aid course is the best way of getting this nailed as there is a recommended technique.

Home security

Making your home as safe as possible, especially when your kid starts toddling, by putting safety catches on cupboards, fixing stair gates, fitting fireguards and ensuring the bookcase won't fall when your child starts climbing up it will narrow down the odds of you ever having to put your first aid skills to use.

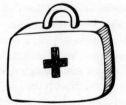

Milestone 39

Kids' party time
Age: second birthday onwards

Throwing or attending birthday parties for kids dominates your
life as a parent, or so it seems. Often, it's like a step back in time
to an age when bartering was common currency – you constantly
find yourself buying gifts for kids you've never met because their
parents bought a gift for your child. The calendar on the fridge
soon resembles a school register as it fills up with the names of
parties your four-year-old social butterfly is invited to. A few
hard-and-fast rules for parties – gleaned from dads with differing
experiences but who did at least attend a kids' bash or two –
are listed below.

Set your clock
Don't let a party dominate your weekend – unless you're a guest of
a very generous host. If the party is at your place then set a party
duration. For under-fives, kick it off at noon and have them out by 3
p.m. – plenty of time to wear them out, but not you.

Parent is the plus-one
Depending on the age range (from toddling–18+), parents will often
drop their child at your party and run like the clappers to rekindle
lost elements of their life for an hour or two while you're their
no-cost childminder. Either insist that it's a party for parents too
(providing the required refreshments to ensure that they stay) or at
least get the phone number for the mum or dad of the child who's
possibly going to excitedly puke Wotsits on to your sofa before
the day's out.

Split the duties

Even in our more egalitarian working world it's still the case that the mums of school children will often know each other while dads commonly only meet at events like this. Slapping name badges on all the guests – Post-it style, not the type you get at a sales conference – will break down barriers and enable you to delegate other dads to do tasks instead of letting them all gather in the kitchen, down your beer and talk football.

Set your menu

In the past, kids' parties took up a whole street and featured a staple of white bread corner sandwiches with indeterminate ingredients, fizzy pop, cake and crisps. You ate these or nothing at all. Today's fare must feature vegan, gluten-free, lactose- and dairy-less, halal, kosher and definitely no E-numbers. Along with low- or no-sugar juices. All should be labelled, nuts should be avoided or you should know the emergency procedure to treat a child who reacts badly to them.

Give party bags a pass

Modern etiquette among the parents of children who are barely off the umbilical cord is to hand out a party bag at the end of the event to all the kids who attended. In time, this escalates into an arms race whereby each host tries to out-gift the last one with more lavish packs of environmentally unsound plastic toys and bulk-buy sweets. Be the bigger man here and break this parcel farce if you can.

If your budget allows you can always book a venue that specialises in throwing kids' parties – and includes entertainers, magicians or clowns doing the job so you don't have to.

Milestone 40

First-time tantrums
Age: 24 months–four years

When your kid first kicks off a tantrum in your company it can be a quite unnerving experience. Suddenly, they don't seem anything like your otherwise happy-go-lucky little toddler. Screaming, shouting, running off, holding their breath, lashing out, biting, kicking or dropping to the ground and performing a 'stranded turtle' dance on their back puts them in a whole new light. It's often a very public performance – usually at a time when you really don't need it to happen – and it's why the term 'terrible twos' has its place in parenting folklore.

On the whole, tantrums are born of frustration. He or she wants to communicate something but hasn't yet developed the language or copy skills to get this across. Remember, too, that just like speaking, walking and peeing in the potty instead of on the sofa, they're still learning and in this case it's learning how to control their emotions and how to deal with being upset. So, the odd upset is inevitable. Tantrum tactics that dads have employed with varying degrees of success include:

- Give a warning. To prevent a meltdown when it's time to let another kid go on the Noddy car at the supermarket let them know that they have 'one more minute' or 'last go'. Prepare them for a transition – 'one more story then bedtime' – in whatever activity they're doing and they'll often accept it painlessly.
- Change the setting. When a meltdown erupts, try removing them from the immediate vicinity – which you'll no doubt want to do when they're screaming down the whole 80-seater restaurant – such as outside, to the toilet or to sit in the car. Wait until they've stopped bawling, then explain to them – calmly – why their

behaviour isn't acceptable. Combining words and actions and being consistent will stop 'tantrums' being seen as an option for your kid.
- Give them choices. Put the ball in their court sometimes. 'What do you want to put on first – shoes or hat?' Tantrums are also a by-product of them wanting to be more independent – play along with that, but don't reward or give in to a screaming fit just for the sake of an easy life.

Arguing with a two-year-old won't make the tantrum stage pass any quicker. Aim to keep calm, kneel down to their level – if you're towering above them they feel it's even harder to communicate, and scream louder – and aim to correct them instead of telling them off. Be aware that the parent who's with their child the most will witness tantrums more frequently. This can make it seem like they 'only kick off' when they're 'with mum' or 'with dad' – in reality, it's just the luck of the draw.

Milestone 41

First time on a plane
Age: one week–four years

Your child taking flight for the first time can go one of two ways: mellow and without incident or complete meltdown, depending on factors such as their age, your destination and how they cope with the ear-popping discomfort of it all.

Plane seating
Depending on the length of your journey and age of your baby you may be taking them in a car seat carrier that's strapped into a plane seat – airlines can and do supply carrycots and child seats (from birth up to two years old) free of charge. You should reserve these when booking and be aware that they can be subject to availability on board the aircraft on the day.

Lap chance
You can also take an infant on your lap – strapped in using a special extension seat belt that the cabin crew provide. Again, the length of the flight and the weight of your baby will need serious consideration before you make a call on this.

Pack snacks
Always check with the airline what you can and can't take in the cabin when it comes to liquids, formulas, medication and snacks. 'A bag with lots of pockets for easy access – containing your baby's special comfort toy, nappies and warm layers – is essential,' says Emily Jones, cabin crew for Emirates Airlines.

Take toys
Bring a mix of old and new toys with you and make a game of giving the toys out by wrapping them up and asking your children to guess

what's inside. Think stacking cups and anything that you can 'hide' other small toys inside.

Pushchair luggage

Check with the airline but if your child is old enough for a pushchair, at most airports you can usually take the small, fully collapsible lightweight pushchair/stroller to the aircraft door and collect it from there at the end of the flight. (It will be put in the hold). Larger pushchairs and travel systems can be taken to the departure gate but collected from the baggage carousel. (Hopefully.)

Baby bedtimes

Try to create a comfortable sleep environment by using eye shades for children and covering any light sources for babies (e.g. put a blanket over the handset lights). Also think about the length of your flight and changing of time zones, as well as how long you will stay at your destination to schedule naps where needed. If possible, try to keep children on as close to their usual sleeping times as you can, as if they need to adjust to a new time zone it is better to make that adjustment once you have reached your destination.

Air rage

Infants, just like adults, find air travel uncomfortable. As a parent, the last thing you want is your child crying in a confined space, though other passengers might not realise this and insist on complaining about your crying baby. Let them know that you're doing your best for your child – whose comfort is your priority – and ignore their complaints.

Milestone 42

Reading to your child

Age: from day one but from 12–18 months you start getting responses to questions like 'where's the doggie?'

It's never too early to start reading to your child. Fathers-to-be are told to read aloud to their partner's belly during the pregnancy so that the baby in the womb can get familiarised with dad's voice. In reality, reading with your kid is more likely to begin with 'baby books' – colourful and full of touchy-feely textures – when they're on your lap, before moving on to bedtime stories, educational books, comics and magazines.

How, when and what you read to your kid is down to you – making sure you do is the key. Research published in the *British Journal of Educational Psychology* into the role of early father involvement and its impact upon children's educational attainment showed 'a positive relationship between the amounts of literacy fathers engage in for their personal use and their children's reading test'. Dads who are seen to be reading a lot around the home – books, newspapers, *Viz*, etc. – send out a positive sign to their children that it's an enjoyable thing to do.

Be a character dad

Reading in a different voice, putting on funny accents, changing words deliberately to see if your kid spots what you've done – all help bring a story to life and make reading time a fun activity your kid will want to do. It's one that doesn't cost you a packet, either.

Repeat 'til fade

When your child's just learning to speak, regularly reading the same story can help with language development and memory. After a few readings of the favourite story they'll become familiar with words and speech patterns.

Throw out a few questions

As your child gets older, try enhancing a story with a few open questions linked to the narrative – 'If a Tiger came to tea at our house what do you think he'd eat?' – which can open up whole new conversations.

Go on a book hunt

Taking your child to the library or bookshop and letting them choose books – even ones that are out of their age range but they just like the look of – will help establish reading and books as being something fun and part of their independence.

READ IT AND REAP

According to a study entitled 'Why Fathers Matter To Their Children's Literacy' by the National Literacy Trust, time-pressured dads reported reading as a major way to develop a unique relationship with their children, while University of Sussex research shows that dads reading to their kids experienced relaxed muscle tension and decreased heart rate within six minutes of turning pages.

Milestone 43

Choosing your first family pet
Age: 12 months onwards

Getting a family pet is a wonderful lesson in nurturing, trust and picking up poo – especially when your kid is old enough to share some of the care. It teaches your child all about responsibility, gives them an insight into nature and is as good a way as any to find out that they're allergic to the labradoodle you just paid through the nose for.

It can be fun and fulfilling – until the day comes when you must break the bad news to them. Telling your nipper that Flipper the goldfish no longer swims with the fishes requires tact and compassion. Here's an estimated time of departure chart so that you'll roughly know when the time will come to break the news ...

Essential pet info

Pet	Average lifespan in years	*Guinness Book of Records* lifespan	Insurance cover
Cat	10–15	25+	Y
Dog	(L) 8–12, (S) 15–20	25+	Y
Tortoise	30	123+	Theft only
Parrot	80	110+	Tracker fitted?
Mouse	1–2	5	Home electrics/ wiring cover

Pet	Average lifespan in years	*Guinness Book of Records* lifespan	Insurance cover
Rabbit	6–10	14+	Fully comp*
Lizard	3 (chameleon)	30 (gecko)	Y
Gerbil/ hamster	2–5 years	5 years & 1 month	N
Goldfish	12	25+	Only if the fairground offers it

*As a father of a kid who had rabbits I can vouch for how expensive the vet bills can be from first-hand experience. Unattended, rabbits can develop 'fly strike' – a maggot-ridden infection of the anus that looks and smells as bad as it sounds. Cost to repair = £600 ($725).

How to break the bad news ...

1. Remember Fido's name when announcing his death (applies to relatives also).
2. Avoid euphemisms such as 'put to sleep' – it can confuse your kid as to what sleep really is. Explain gently that Fido died and he's not coming back.
3. Encourage them to talk about their feelings – let them know it is OK to be sad or cry. But don't be surprised if they've not really grasped the concept of death yet either.
4. Let your kid say their goodbyes to help understand that Fido won't be coming back.
5. Don't think that getting another puppy is the easy option. Take a break, make some time to grieve and enjoy life for a few weeks without dog hair and smelling of Chum before bringing another animal into your lives.

Milestone 44

Finding out that your kid's a fussy eater

Age: 18 months onwards

'Discerning tastes' is how we describe this as an adult, or else having a 'mild intolerance of ...' As a kid it's called being a 'fussy eater' or 'picky about their food'. Basically, it's not something we grow out of – we just change our tastes as we grow older. What your kid loves as a two-year-old – milk, pineapple, bogey – they may detest by the time they're five. You'll start noticing it during the weaning stage – but more so when eating out, staying with friends or relatives, at other kids' parties – and suddenly at home mealtimes when they just start leaving stuff they don't like.

Demanding toddlers and weaning babies will try a food up to 20 times before finally deciding if they like it or not – frustrating when you've just bought a year's supply worth of their ex-favourite food from Costco. But there are ways of dealing with a 'picky eater' who won't touch some foods unless it's to throw them at you.

Eat with them
It sounds pretty basic but putting food in front of them while you're off doing something much more interesting can put them off eating generally. Sit down to eat with them – even if it's just a snack for you. As they get older involve them in the food prep and cooking – it'll raise their appetite, too.

Turn off the screen
Don't get into the habit of feeding them with the TV on. Instead, use that as a reward for when their plate has been cleared.

Daddy's sauce

Fun up food if need be. Coating the vegetables with healthy dips and sauces, making faces on the plate and giving small portions – and plenty of praise when they finish them up – will make mealtimes enjoyable.

Let them loose

It will be messy, but as soon as they can, let them feed themselves. It's more likely that they'll eat more when it's done at their pace. Avoid strong flavours and spices while their taste buds are still developing – finger foods like sandwiches, cheese, breadsticks and hummus, small sausages, vegetable sticks, pieces of fruit, fish fingers and a few chips are staples of the toddler tableaux.

When to seek help

Some days your kid won't have much of an appetite – then they'll be insatiable the next. Their tastes will change, but if you have any worries about the food they're refusing – they will only eat a handful of food types, they shun whole food groups, there's always a trauma at mealtimes – or you think their 'fussy eating' is affecting their growth then it's time to speak to your GP or a specialist child dietician.

Milestone 45

Child tortures family pet
Age: three years

Discovering that you've brought Damien from *The Omen* into this world is an understandably upsetting time for all right-thinking, upstanding and compassionate parents. The clues to your infant's penchant for pain, sadism and pure evil will most likely be evident in their treatment of your pet cat, or someone else's pet cat, or the family guinea pig/hamster/faithful old Labrador, or ducks on the pond, petting zoo rabbits, the school gerbils, a feral pigeon or other children who come within kicking range.

Being cruel towards dumb animals isn't normal – but at toddling age it's, well, a bit more common. Your kid might start teasing, hitting or pulling the tail of your cat or dog. Without knowing better, or because they're bored, or because they think it's a toy, or because they've seen it done by someone else, they can make life hell for some pets until you step in. If this sounds familiar, you need to:

- Keep watch. Don't leave the pets alone with your child, especially at baby and toddler age – or at least give the cat an escape route from the kid who's high tailing it after them.
- Teach them to be tame. Show your son or daughter how to be kind to your kitty – pointing out that when you're gentle with the pet they're happy and soon retract those claws.
- Give them a lesson. Show your son or daughter how similar your pets are to him or her, in order to tap into their feelings of empathy. Teach them to read the cat's body language – recognising that purring means the cat enjoys it but the tail swishing and fluffing up and teeth being shown mean it's time to back off.

When to be concerned

At toddler age, it's understandable that children don't always differentiate between animals and toys. They're also a bit clumsy, heavy-handed and curious. But if you start seeing your child behaving badly towards your pets when they're well into school years – six and onwards – and do understand that animals have feelings and that it's not OK to hurt them, then it may be time to get some professional guidance on this.

If you witness your kid abusing animals in their teens it's unlikely they're doing it solely for kicks. There's plenty of evidence to show that this kind of activity can stem from peer group pressure – part of an initiation rite – or because the child enjoys the sense of control it gives them. There are going to be deeper-rooted issues to this behaviour to confront and investigate further.

Milestone 46

Family member dies
Age: five onwards

Helping your children cope with grief is especially tough when you as adults are also struggling to come to terms with the loss of a loved one. Losing a grandparent, parent, sibling or close friend will hit most families hard and children at almost any age will feel a sense of loss, but for teenagers – going through the transition from the security of childhood to the independence of adulthood – it can be especially traumatic.

When it's a child's first experience it can help if Dad or Mum talks them through what has happened and what will happen next. Providing some answers where you can will ease their anxiety – letting them decide what they might be able to do at this time to help them feel better is vital. This can include talking to them about ...

Down time
If you don't want them to attend a funeral or memorial service – or they don't want to go – give each other a chance to explain why. It may help to find another way for them to mark what's happened or commemorate the passing of someone they love.

Wake up
If you are taking your child to the funeral or wake, prepare them for what to expect. If you're involved in the planning of the service include your son or daughter in the discussions – they may have a particularly poignant way of saying farewell that will mean a lot to them and others attending the service. Offer them the chance to participate, but don't force.

Good grief

Adolescents may find it odd to be asked about 'how they're coping' or 'if they're feeling OK' at this time. They – like you – will still be trying to get their head around what has happened if a close friend or relative has gone. Be prepared for a flood of emotions from them (more so than usual anyway), or an outpouring of angst (ditto), or even for them to seemingly be carrying on regardless. All of these are normal reactions. Some of us can feel guilty because we're not in tears all the time and instead are coping OK.

It may help to share your feelings with your children at this time, too – it can encourage them to open up and reassure them that it's normal for the pain of grief to come and go over time. Where possible, keep to your family routines and as much normality as you can – letting them know not to feel guilty about feeling happy and having fun at times, too.

Milestone 47

First time you put your kid on a bike

Age: four onwards

The recommended age for first teaching a kid to ride a bike is four–six years old. Before that they may well have been whizzing around on a scooter or a balance bike, but once their co-ordination has developed to the point where they're comfortable pushing the pedals then it's time to move on to the tricks, tips and etiquette of the road.

But let's not jump ahead of ourselves here. According to the bike specialist Isla Rowntree, who taught her kids to ride (and thanks to her Isla Bikes range now helps get children of all ages on to wheels for the first time), starting out is easier if you follow a few rules.

Begin with balance

The best way to learn the balance required for cycling is to start with a balance bike. Avoid using stabilisers on kids' bikes because they don't allow your child to get a natural feel for balance and turning. If a balance bike isn't available, it is possible to get your child learning about the feel and balance of a bike by removing the pedals and lowering the saddle of a normal pedal bike. They can then push themselves along with the security of being able to get their feet on the floor. If they're using the bike as a balance bike it is important to have the saddle low enough that the child can get their feet flat on the floor with a slight bend in the knee.

Time to pedal

Once they're confident and happy balancing on their own you can introduce the pedals. First, get their saddle height correct for pedalling; this is different to the saddle height for a balance bike. The ideal saddle height for pedalling is for them to be on the balls of their feet when in the seated position. It is tempting to go lower to start with so that they can get their feet easily on the floor, but this hinders the pedalling action and can make balancing much more difficult as their knees will be coming up to their chest.

Flat and firm
It's tempting to choose grass as the place to start them out riding, but that makes learning to ride quite difficult because they will have to push hard on the pedals to get the bike moving. Find a spot that's quiet (no cars) and on firm ground – tarmac is ideal. The ground should be flat, so they don't pick up too much speed.

Give them a hand
Hold on to your child from behind, under the armpits; make sure you don't hold on to the handlebars or the back of the saddle as this takes control away from the child, meaning they don't get the necessary steering feedback. Let them learn how the bike reacts when they are leaning. Encourage them to look up, let go of their brakes and pedal. Walk forwards (still holding them under the armpits) and slowly release your grip as they gain confidence, correcting their direction if they go offline.

When you're showing them how to use the brakes get them to walk with their bike at first and apply the brakes so they get the gist of how they work – and not to squeeze too tightly.

Take it slowly
Teaching your kid to ride should be a fun experience for all involved – unlike most of the cycling they'll do on UK roads once they reach adulthood ... If you can, avoid teaching them too much in one go. Let them master the basics before showing them the wheelies and endos you used to do as a kid.

Milestone 48

Screening a babysitter

Age: two months onwards but more likely when they're infants

When the time feels right to leave your bundle of joy with a professional carer, your role is more than simply agreeing a fee, the time you'll be back and throwing in a free pizza. You also need the skillset to determine if the babysitter is nurturing, engaging or people trafficking.

Tap one up

As for home delivery dinners and taxis to your door, there's an app for babysitters these days. Options like Yoopies, Bambino and the rather 'street' UrbanSitter offer up local au pairs, housewives and moonlighting nursery teachers along with registered childminders and students earning cash by keeping one eye on their studies and another one on your baby. These platforms pair up suitable sitters with parents desperate to leave the house. Rates vary according to experience, locale and time duration.

Seek out the magic circle

Babysitting circles pre-date the digital era. They're usually informal groups of new parents – be it from antenatal groups, swim clubs, crèches or a local community hub – who take turns looking after each other's children. The advantages are that they're friends, they have kids the same age as yours, and budget may not be an issue. (These often work on a reciprocal basis: you wipe my baby's bum and I'll wipe yours.) The disadvantages are that they're friends – so without a formal agreement some may take advantage of another's good nature – and that you do have to wipe another baby's bum.

Go with the pros

Professional registered childminders found through national organisations such as Sitters put you in touch with a trusted, local network of babysitters. With some organisations there's a membership fee on top of the payment for a sitter – bear in mind, too, that fees can (and really should) go up on 'high demand' nights, such as New Year's Eve or Valentine's Day.

And a few other things ...

- Whichever route you go down there's no legal age babysitters have to be, but think carefully about using anyone under 16. Any younger and they might not be mature enough – or have the authority – to be in charge.
- Also, get referrals from people who've used them as a babysitter before.
- Ask the babysitter how they'd deal with situations like your child refusing to go to bed.
- Agree the fee, what time you'll be home and whether or not you're paying a taxi fare for the sitter to get home afterward.
- Before you leave the house, check that you have each other's phone numbers and agree any perks (e.g. they can help themselves to the biscuits but not the Bacardi ...)

103

Milestone 49

Panic that you're not cutting it as a parent

Age: day one onwards

When you go through the monumental life change of becoming a dad, it can trigger a wide range of physical and psychological reactions. Around one in five women report feeling low and unable to cope as new mums, while official estimates say one in 10 new dads are likely to feel the same. Mental health campaigners like Mark Williams, author of *Daddy Blues*, believe the figure is much higher. 'Both my wife and I suffered with postnatal depression following the very traumatic birth of our child,' explains Mark.

Because of the fatiguing nature of new parenthood it's often easy to miss or dismiss the symptoms of postnatal depression, which can include:

- feeling low in mood
- lethargy – not wanting to do anything or take an interest in the outside world
- feelings of guilt about not coping, or about not loving your baby enough
- having anxiety or panic attacks
- greater dependence on drink or drugs to cope.

'If a new father feels that his partner is struggling to cope or may be suffering with postnatal depression he could talk to the health visitor and get an appointment with the doctor,' suggests Mark. 'For someone suffering with postnatal depression the simplest of tasks can some days seem like a mountain. As the new dad you'll most likely be the first to witness her symptoms – even if you don't know exactly what they are.'

Reassure her that feeling depressed and tearful are not signs of her being a 'bad mother' or one who's not coping. She may be reluctant to speak to a health professional about it, so dads can help by discussing the specific behaviours and symptoms. Fathers, too, need to be aware of the symptoms of postnatal depression in themselves and seek help for the sake of themselves and their new family.

Mark found help via counselling, cognitive behavioural therapy and mindfulness – but only after suffering a breakdown. His advice to parents who recognise the symptoms is to accept that they're not alone in feeling this way and that there are organisations that can help confront and combat the effects of depression.

Milestone 50

Making more time for your kids
Age: 12 months onwards

Research shows that 50 per cent of British parents with a child under 18 say they would like to spend more time together, while 60 per cent of parents admit that when they do spend time with their children, it's usually doing something non-active. The same cheery studies reveal that 'quality' family time is a mere 34 minutes a day on average.

Making more time for the children is tough – especially when your parental leave is up and you're both back to putting in extra hours to feed the extra mouths. For some dads, though, the arrival of a child can prompt a drastic rethink of how they work and use their time. Striking that balance between earning a living and raising a child can involve some or all of the following ...

Take care
Depending on the type of work you do, you could consider childcare facilities that double as co-working spaces – found through companies like Bloom. These allow you to cut down on your commute, saving precious family time at the beginning and end of every day. Shared spaces also allow parents to check in on their kids while simultaneously allowing for some separation.

Put your child first
While some childcare facilities, day care groups or schools with an after-school club may help you juggle your time or commute a little better, don't make its convenience the number one reason for choosing it. Make sure your child is happy and safe there – if it's en

route to work and extends the time you get with them a little then that's a bonus.

Keep a daddy diary
Set up a family calendar or get into the habit of logging family duties, school holidays, sports days, team practice or parents' evenings in your app to avoid clashing work schedules with your children's activities.

Set shut-off times
Log off from the laptop or phone and remove any work-related distractions at the end of the day so that you can spend the time your kids are awake indulging them. You can always catch up on social media or emails when they've gone to bed.

Be first up
Kids typically act as your alarm clock when they're pre-school age but to spend more fun time with them it's worth getting up before they do – preparing yourself for work and their stuff for nursery or school – and where possible sharing breakfast in a more relaxed manner.

Take up takeaways

As fun and healthy as it is to make meals for the family, when your time is at a premium and you want to play with your kids before they go to bed look into having meal delivery kits – Abel & Cole, Prep Perfect and others – there's a veritable feast of these online. In short, just have takeaways or ready meals more often while your kids are young.

Milestone 51

Auditing your essential dad skills
Age: five years onwards

'I just had to apologise to a toy giraffe and kiss a race car
good night – parenting is weirder than I thought it'd be ...'

Dadsnet

I'm not one to stereotype here but part and parcel of being a hands-on,
influential, inspirational, instructive, knowledgeable and nurturing
full-time father means having a set of 'dad skills' that you can reliably
perform and use to save the day when the need calls for it. We're not
talking about rewiring the house, hot-wiring the car or even getting
the lid off the peanut butter (though that one is a given), just most of
these everyday heroic acts:

- Create toys out of junk – turning a wet bank holiday into an
  adventure using just the cardboard box that the new TV came in,
  some kitchen paper inner tubes and something Mum will go nuts
  about when she finds out you've used it to create a dolls house,
  space station, magical fortress.
- Undo tough knots in school ties or shoelaces.
- Pitch a tent ... before it starts raining.
- Fix a bike puncture.
- Tread on lego shoeless without swearing.
- Perform a mesmerising magic trick using just body parts.
- Have ingenious methods of getting your child off to sleep – hypnotic
  sing-and-carry routines, dusting off your more obscure vinyl,
  dangling them at a weird angle. This is vital when your partner is
  despairing and needs you to step in and perform your party trick.
- Upload or download films, music and computer games without
  getting ruffled.
- Put up a gazebo for a kids' garden party ... before it rains.

- Set up and fill a paddling pool ... before it rains.
- Erect a windbreak on a beach ... before it rains.
- Give lessons in life to your kids via a rearview mirror.
- Build an epic sandcastle that other beach users envy.
- Have a sport, game or activity your kid never manages to beat you at.
- Drive while eating crisps.
- Explode an empty crisp packet to make Mum jump.
- Respond to every 'why?' question with a different answer.
- Mind control – make your toddler get back into bed, give Nanny a kiss or let the patiently waiting child have a go on the Postman Pat ride outside the supermarket without a scene that can only be quelled with an exorcism.
- Blow up balloons ... Loads of balloons.
- Light, maintain and cook to an edible standard on a barbecue.
- Keep a secret from Mum (by forgetting you were told it in the first place).
- Have a specialist subject – they maybe can't turn to you for help with calculus, statistics or Cantonese, but when it comes to the names of dinosaurs, Vietnam War films or the grounds of all 92 English football league teams you're a mastermind.
- Construct a flatpack 'bunk' bed with desk beneath it.
- Climb ladders or trees to retrieve balls, kites, drones, kids.
- Autopiloting: performing nocturnal chores such as feeding babies or changing wet bedding and pyjamas without waking anyone – even yourself.
- Light a fire.
- Toss pancakes.
- Teach a child to float in the pool.
- Play make-believe with other dads.
- Carry a child on your shoulders without 'crowning' them on a branch.
- Detect and pick the biggest, juiciest blackberries.
- Refit a bicycle chain.
- Get glue off of anything it shouldn't be stuck to.
- Have a ready supply of batteries, lightbulbs, fuses and glue.
- Mimic any animal – for the purposes of bedtime stories you're able to move seamlessly from making the noise of a moo cow and a quacking duck to a nuthatch, lemur, Gruffalo or Thomson's gazelle (mating call).
- Clean boots or shoes so they look like new again.
- Secure things to a car roof.
- Take stuff to the dump.
- Find a dock leaf to ease a nettle sting.

Milestone 52

Requesting flexible working time
Age: 12 months onwards

Flexible working is a wonderful opportunity for parents to manage the work–life balance a lot better once kids come along. By changing their start and finish times, working from home more often or doing 'compressed hours' parents can get more involved in family life and be there to help bring up their children. That's the theory.

In reality, out of nearly 40 per cent of working dads who requested a change in their working hours since becoming fathers, almost half were refused, while only one in five dads who request to work from home are granted permission, according to the Daddilife/Deloitte Millennial Dad Study 2019.

'Applying for flexible work has generally been perceived to be the domain of the returning/working mum and many dads are put off by giving people the impression that they care more about something outside of work,' explains Simon Gregory, co-founder of GPS Return, who help full-time parents return to work. If you're thinking about applying for flexible work Simon has some ideas on how to get it.

Know what you want
What's going to work best for you and your family? Doing a school drop-off three days a week? Taking every Friday off? Remote working three days a week? 'Don't be afraid to get creative, a nine-day fortnight works really well for a single dad friend of mine, whereas compressing four days into three works perfectly for another,' explains Simon.

Do your homework
Talk to friends and colleagues who work flexibly to find out a bit more about the process, what to expect and objections you might face. 'Informally sound out your manager about flexible working

over a coffee,' suggests Simon. 'Gauge their reaction, take note of any objections/concerns and work possible solutions into your plan.'

Make a plan

'Build a business plan showing how your flexi working will affect your team and what you intend to do to minimise any risk,' suggests Simon. 'Put yourself in the shoes of the biggest critic to think of the objections they will have. Then work this into your plan.'

Prepare to fight

It is highly likely that you will have to fight harder to get the flexibility you need than do your female counterparts. 'Society, as a whole, isn't quite as ready to accept men requesting flexible work as women so we do have to work a bit harder to achieve it and you will be at the receiving end of "banter" and questions over your commitment to your career, so prepare yourself and push through it,' says Simon.

Make it work

When you succeed, you will be watched. 'No more Facebook, no more time to chat about Saturday's game and no more long lunches on a Friday, you have to be on it 100 per cent of the time,' warns Simon. 'Show that you can do everything you said you would in your business plan and more. There will be people waiting and watching to point a finger, but, more importantly, there will also be other dads watching to see how you get on. But more than this, you owe it to yourself and your family to make it work so that you can be both the parent and the professional you want to be.'

The school years...

At last! Your child's learning, education and social development are no longer solely down to you ...

Milestone 53

Dad's first day at the school gate
Age: four upwards

Whether it's at the school gate, in the playground, on the sports field (remember those?) or in the side-road-cum-parent's-car-park, whichever place you go to drop off and pick up your child at school can seem like an intimidating one for the uninitiated dad. Even if you visited the school before signing your kid up to it and attended a pre-school briefing, nothing quite prepares you for the rituals of the school run and dynamics of the school gate.

It's no different for new school mums either of course – which is why you'll find kindred spirits among both men and women, eventually – but there are a few things that you should know as a new school dad ...

You can't *just* leave...
Lunch, book bag, books to go in the book bag, games kit, homework diary, coloured pencils, pencil case, water bottle, fruit snack, school jumper, sun cream, sun hat, raincoat, school pet, reply slip to confirm attendance at school trip/after-school club/parents' evening ... Check! Child? Ooops!

Dads don't talk
It'll take a school social event, a nod of acknowledgement during the dad's race on sports day or a close bond between your kid and theirs before two dads will strike up a conversation in the playground. School mums are often accused of being 'cliquey' but they just strike up school-gate friendships a lot more quickly than most dads.

Say 'yes'

Parent Teacher Association (PTA) member, school trip helper, 'Father Christmas', school governor, sports team assistant, reading mentor, manning the tombola, being the goalie in 'Beat the Goalie' or even 'parking warden'* – you *will* be asked to perform at least one of these duties if you're a regular male face at the school gate.

Other kids attend this school ...

... And you'll be expected to know their names, their parents' names, when these kids have birthdays and whether your partner approves of these kids being friends with your child or not. Learn and revise, as you will be tested almost constantly on these topics.

If all this seems overwhelming and you're only at the nursery stage, then get used to it. The average age for a child to start going to school without parents in tow is 12.

*(This involves donning a hi-vis vest and getting abuse from other parents who want to park as close to the school as possible.)

> **DAD FACTS: School holidays dominate your diary – and yet they still creep up on you**
>
> One moment you're busily carrying on as working parents, dropping junior at primary school and heading off to the serious stuff – the next you've got SIX WHOLE WEEKS with no one else to look after your child except you. (See also astronomical increase in holiday costs and air fares.)

Milestone 54

Getting to know your kid's friends
Age: four onwards

At around four years old your child will start playing *with* other children as opposed to just playing alongside them. They build friendships now, learning each other's names and asking questions about what they like and don't like in order to identify common bonds. There's even a fascinating TV show called *The Secret Life of 4-Year-Olds* in the UK and Australia that observes these interactions via hidden cameras. Each episode lasts an hour – which is, coincidentally, about as much as any parent can take of other people's kids in one go.

It's useful to get to know your kid's friends – going beyond just asking your child why they're no longer playing with 'the ginger one'. Here's a few dad dos and don'ts when getting pally ...

Don't make them 'your' friends
Avoid the urge to be 'cool' dad by getting all matey and informal with your kid's friends. They'll find it awkward, your child will hate it and it'll blur the boundaries when it comes to having to ban them from your house.

Do tap them up for ideas
New parents share ideas or what they've learned during the baby years with other parents via postnatal groups, forums, social events etc. But by the time the kids are at school there's less of that group chat. Your kid's friends, however, will unwittingly spill the beans on such issues as what time they go to bed, what their parents make for tea, where the cheapest holiday destination is this summer and so on, without you even having to ask chatty kid's mum and dad.

Don't be surprised if you only see them once

One week they're your child's BFF (best friend forever, in case you didn't know) – the next they're off the birthday party list and never seen again. Kids are picking stuff up and dropping it all the time as they grow – bad habits, music lessons and friends included.

Do keep opinions to yourself

The quickest way of ensuring that your child becomes inseparable from a friend of theirs who you can't stand is by airing your opinion of them. Equally, avoid heaping too much praise on a friend of theirs who you consider a great positive influence, a role model, or 'really nice' – that'll be the last you see of them, too.

Don't change the rules

If you don't let your kids watch TV during meals or play Fortnite before their homework is done then stick to your rules, no matter how much they 'do things differently at Lucy/Leo's house'.

Do swap details

Get contact details from your kid's friend's parents. Have a chat with their parents ahead of a sleepover to see what they do and don't allow their child to watch, eat or stay up beyond. (It'll prevent an awkward call after your nine-year-old's best friend tells their mum about the 12-hour *The Walking Dead* binge viewing that you allowed ...)

Do keep up with their friendships

In their tweens and teenage years, friends seem to become more important to your child than family. Your child may go to extreme lengths to try to fit in with their peers – making some bad choices or getting into risky situations. Knowing their close friends – and their parents – can help you keep them safe without them feeling smothered.

Milestone 55

Helping them overcome shyness
Age: four onwards

Shyness in children often comes to light when they're first in social situations beyond the immediate family – such as when they start nursery or school, where teachers may notice it. They may seem nervous or afraid around other kids, electing to play on their own and watching other kids play, but always reluctant to join in.

It's not uncommon in children – or adults for that matter – and not a major problem unless it develops into a more chronic form of social anxiety. Shy people live and cope with it. Behavioural genetics experts at Kings College London estimate that about 30 per cent of shyness as a trait is down to genetics and the rest comes about as a response to the environment.

If you want to help your child deal with their shyness, without making them feel pressured or putting them into situations where matters are just made worse try the following.

A favourite activity as a take-off point
If your child has a particular activity they enjoy, are good at and put a lot of focus into – playing a certain game, looking after a pet, doing a sport – use that as a base. Having another friend or young relative come on a playdate with that activity as a focal point could help. Your child will be more comfortable with what they're doing, maybe even feeling like telling the friend about it and interacting with them.

Stick with one-on-one
If your child isn't good in crowds then one-on-one play sessions, days out and trips to the park can help them develop their social interaction skills in a way they're happy with. Always let them know what's going

to be happening and give them something to look forward to – don't spring anything on them as a surprise.

Avoid overprotection ...

Don't restrict your child's opportunities to mix and learn social skills, though. Take them to birthday parties and events they may find challenging but give them the option to leave early if they feel uncomfortable. Avoid using 'she's shy' as an excuse or a label. 'She likes to observe what's going on first' works better.

Show them the way...

Specialists who help shy children will use puppets or action figures to role-play social skills. You can try modelling behaviour by doing the same or just saying things like 'Can I play too?' when your child is playing alone.

You won't turn your child into a buzzing socialite overnight but with patience and by praising your child when they do begin to build connections with other kids you can help them find the confidence they need to live with while being a bit more reflective and laid-back than some of their peers.

Milestone 56

Your kid swears for the first time

Age: four and, unfortunately, onwards

When they're around four years old kids develop a love for exploring – hiding behind the sofa, digging around beneath your bed and climbing into boxes. They also start to explore language and enjoy nothing more than testing out new words – to understand their meaning or because they just like the way they roll off the tongue, or the reaction they get from others. Swearing can be an offshoot of this, as they play with words they've usually overheard.

How to handle it

What to do about swearing? Ignore it. Tricky I know, especially when it's a public outburst – but if their playground profanity is attention seeking then this is often the best way to stop it. Only if they continue to swear – or you want to use the opportunity of them mispronouncing a word to give them a bit of insight into 'words we don't use' – is it worth picking up on your kid's fondness for coarse language. If you do go down this path, here are a few pearls of wisdom:

- Don't go into details about what the word means – even if they're old enough to understand it. 'That's not a nice word' might be enough, but they're inquisitive types so turn the conversation back and ask them what they think it means.
- At infant age they'll play with insults and swear words – finding terms like 'farty face' hilarious. Telling them that they're not words you want to hear at home might help establish some ground rules around 'not-nice words'.
- As they get older, the reasons for using bad language can be more refined. The best way to counter this seems to be to give

them attention when they *don't* swear (i.e. praise them for being articulate, having a good vocabulary, not offending the vicar etc.). Avoid laughing or encouraging swearing if you don't want to hear it from them.

- If frustration is the cause, it may simply be a case of helping them to achieve whatever it is they're trying to do. Teach them that reacting in a calmer way will help them get what they want.
- Definitely avoid swearing yourself. Some parents opt for inoffensive words instead – 'flip' or 'freaking' – around the house so that the frustration gets vented but no one gets pissed off.

Dad tales

'I'll never forget the day. He was not long past four years old and we had just come back home from a pretty standard day by all accounts – racing cars at nursery while dabbling in his latest Picasso skills. Then he told me about the new word he had heard one of the new kids at class saying. "Daddy, it's called 'fuck'". I nearly choked on my tea. "Pardon!" I said. "Fuck – it's what you say to get people to go away. Sometimes you need to do it with 'off.'" You know that feeling when anger meets shock, meets struggling to not burst out laughing! That was me for a couple of seconds. After I heard more about how that word came to being I told him that that was in fact a very, very bad word, and that he shouldn't be using it. He hadn't said it for six months, and then one day he came home and said, "Daddy there was a new word today..."

Han-Son Lee, father of Max

Milestone 57

Using and perfecting your dad joke repertoire
Age: seven and onwards

'Dad, can you give me a lift?' 'Sure Son, you're a talented kid, and me and Mum are so proud of ya!'

Dad jokes are a worldwide phenomenon it seems. They're not easy to define – but when you hear one you know it's a dad joke. Our kids are unwitting harvesters of dad jokes. Their positive response to Dad's puns in the early days only encourages us fathers to crack on. And that's a good thing. When tension rises in the household and a bit of light relief is required then a dad gag can save the day. According to TV funnyman Clay Nicholls, co-creator of US father's advice channel DadLabs.com, the dad joke plays a vital part in parenting. 'I think these bad jokes are a wonderful kind of teasing – we're playing with the expectations that our kids have of us old people. The best possible result is my 14-year-old daughter trying to conceal a smile at one of my groaners.'

There may even be a scientific reason why we start telling them. Testosterone has been deemed to make male humour generally more aggressive in its tone when compared to the types of jokes that women tell or find funny – according to research published in the *British Medical Journal*. But fatherhood has an adverse effect on testosterone levels. Expectant and new fathers can see their levels of the hormone drop – almost on a par with their bank balance – once there's another mouth to feed. As a result, our jokes may become gentler and less hostile post-kids.

Humour also binds relationships closer and by playing with words in jokes, dads engage their kids in the flexibility of language – encouraging them to think about words, too. The only downside is that jokes are notoriously difficult to remember. So, here are a few to refer to when you need to pull a few funnies out of the hat:

- 'I'll call you later.' 'Why not call me Dad?'
- I love eye jokes – the cornea the better.
- Why did the crab never share? Because he's shellfish.
- Did you hear the rumour about the butter? Well, I'm not going to spread it!
- I wouldn't buy anything with Velcro. It's a total rip-off!
- I keep trying to lose weight ... but it keeps finding me.
- How many tickles does it take to make an octopus laugh? Ten-tickles!
- What do you call a bear without any teeth? A gummy bear!
- I went to buy some camouflage trousers the other day ... but I couldn't find any.
- Have you ever tried to eat a clock? Its very time-consuming.
- Why did the tomato blush? Because it saw the salad dressing.
- What do you call a small mother? A minimum.
- Where do you learn to make ice cream? Sundae school.

Milestone 58

First time at the match
Age: four onwards

It's a rite of passage that has gone down through the years – much like the fortunes of your favourite team. Taking your son or daughter to their first game is an event that will be seared into the memory of your offspring, but not always for the best reasons. They may forget many things over the years but that debut appearance of the team they go on to follow devoutly won't fade. So, it won't require much on your part to make it an outstanding event, but you might want to consider a few factors before kick-off.

Loyal or local?

What's it to be – the team you've supported all your life, or the local club to where your child lives? Chances are they're one and the same, but uprooting for work, love or house prices these days has thrown a spanner into the works when it comes to supporters inheriting their parents' team. Catching your old hometown team when they're playing at the place you live now – with a couple of tickets in the away supporters' section – is one way of blooding your kid into the ways of being an 'exile'.

Grass roots or glory?

Bringing your kid up to have an appreciation for the local non-league, semi-pro or lower-division outfit will give them a good grounding in the culture of the sport you follow. They'll see that it's not just about the rich clubs that are always on TV, and it's a whole lot cheaper to take your child to see that shambles down the road than it is to get a season ticket for the out-of-town glory boys.

Matchday tips

Once you've chosen, a few practical tips to ensure the experience doesn't put your kid off for life are:

- Pack your kit. Snacks, drinks and something warm to wear will keep things comfortable and the cost down.
- Take support. If it's a team you've not followed before or a new ground it pays to go with someone who knows the set-up. A fellow parent who takes their kid regularly can help find the best spot to sit – especially if they're members – and help with getting tickets.
- Pre-match team talk. Warn your child to be prepared for the noise, surging, singing, chanting, foul language and loutish behaviour that their father will engage in.

DAD TALK: First time at a match ...

'Somewhere in my 18-year-old son's bedroom is a Barcelona plastic bag from our trip to Camp Nou. It has all the great stuff he acquired as a little kid, the things I suggested he look after. There are two drum sticks signed by the Beastie Boys after their last ever UK show, autographs from Daniel Craig and Lionel Messi, and definitely in there is a programme from Leeds away to QPR from around 2006. I don't remember the score but I know we lost, we invariably do at Queens Park Rangers, it's a lovely intimate ground but not one Leeds ever get much from. It was Marlais's first ever game. I asked him recently if he remembered it, and he replied "I know it was QPR but I can't remember if it was Leeds (my team) or Arsenal (his)." He was more excited on the day. Not that it had much to do with football. At half-time fifty-odd soldiers engaged in a one-on-one hand-to-hand combat display on gym mats. And then, when a massive black-faced cat walked round the ground I went down and talked it into visiting the box we were in. The mascot was about 7 feet tall and asked to meet the little boy in the box. Marlais couldn't believe it. It took another 8 years or so until he came with me to see us lose away at Charlton to realise that supporting a team could also involve lots of legitimate swearing in chants.'

James Brown, father of Marlais and author of Above Head Height: A Five-a-side Life

Milestone 59

Question time
Age: four onwards

At any point between their nursery years and the end of their time at primary school you will probably have whole days with your son or daughter that will go like this:

'Daddy ... Why is my poo a different colour to my food? Why do people die? What is a fart? Where did I come from? Why is that woman shouting? What is God? How was I made? What does "we can't afford it" mean? What is sex? Is Father Christmas real? Why do I have to go to school? When you die, who will I live with? What came first, dogs or cats? What is "gay"? Why is the sky blue? Why can't I stay up as late as you? Why do tigers have stripes but leopards have spots? Could you win a fight with a tiger? When can I have a mobile phone? Why don't you have much hair on your head? What are ghosts? When can I drive a car? What does "adopted" mean? Why isn't my skin brown? Why does the train keep stopping? Why did you swear at that cyclist? Why are some people fat? How does the internet work? Yeah but what does God look like? Where does the sun go at night-time? Why can't bunny rabbits talk? Why is water wet? Where does wind come from? Why do we have a leap year? Why is blood red? What is infinity? How big is the world? Why doesn't the sky fall down? How do stinging nettles sting me? How do planes fly? How does TV work? Why am I right-handed? Why can't I talk to strangers? Why does Grandad smell funny? What is electricity? How do clouds float? How does a washing machine work? Where have the dinosaurs gone? Why are people's eyes different colours? Why is Mummy crying? How does lightning strike? Why are there so many languages? Why does that man not have a home? What are bogeys? Can't we be rich? Why shouldn't I tell tales? What are there more of, trees or buildings? Why can't we move house? What are dreams? Why can't I have chips every day? Why don't I have a tail? Will I have to go to work? How do telephones work? Are you as rich as the Queen? What colour is white?

Do people die forever? Why does it snow? How are shadows made? What is time? Why is the sea salty? Have I had my lunch? How far away is the moon? Can we live in a castle? Why don't grown-ups go to school? How did people make tools before they had tools? How high can you jump? What is light made of? Why does God let bad things happen? Who do you love the most, me or Mummy? Where do teeth come from? What's the naughtiest thing you've ever done? Could you win a fight with a shark? What's your favourite swear word? Why is it called "the moon"? Have you ever taken drugs? What else do anteaters eat? Why are pizzas round-shaped? What does the sky taste of? Why don't fish have fur? Why do you snore? How do mirrors work? Why do we need money to buy things? Why do snails like rain? Do you believe in God? Why do I have freckles? What about a fight with a tiger AND a shark?'

Cherish this inquisitiveness no matter how incessant it gets. When they hit 15 and the only communication you have involves grunts or one-word text replies, you'll remember these days fondly.

One study among 1500 parents found that children ask their parents questions from as early as 6 a.m. and continue to do so until bedtime at 8 p.m. Dads are often subjected to more questions than mums – on average your kid will ask 413 questions a week. Be prepared to face some pretty searching ones along the way. You'll have your own views on how best to address the real awkward ones but these tips may help ...

Where do babies come from?

With any questions of a sexual nature, try gauging how much your kid knows or what they think they know before giving your reply; it may surprise or at least entertain you finding out their thoughts on this. 'Where do you think they come from ...?' is a straightforward enough response and it'll help to clarify exactly what they're asking you.

Keep your answers honest and simple – avoiding stuff about birds, bees or storks delivering babies to rooftops, but also avoiding too much detail unless they ask more questions.

Don't put them off asking you about these topics – if you can't answer on the spot, ask them to ask you again later. Explaining that making babies is something that grown-ups can do and that your child might not understand right now helps prepare the ground a little. Another option is 'Good question, let's find out together' and then get hold of one of the many books written by child psychologists or agony aunts that provide answers to 'kids' toughest questions'. Such advice may include:

- Tell a toddler that babies grow inside Mummy's tummy.
- At early school age they may ask 'How do babies come out of Mummy's tummy?' In which case a bit of basic, age-appropriate biology may be required, calling up the terms 'birth canal' and 'vagina'.
- When your 10-year-old starts asking you it's probably time to bite the bullet. Again, sound out how much they know at this point, and try to clear up any misunderstandings they may have about sex in the process, before giving them the truth in as matter-of-fact a way as you can muster.

What's going to happen to me?

Television news, world events and school discussions, as well as family tragedies, often trigger a barrage of questions for our kids, especially when they're trying to allay their own fears. You may not be able to explain why a terrorist act has happened or why Nanny isn't going to be around any more and in these situations you don't necessarily need to. Your child's reasons for asking will probably stem from fears around their own safety, such as 'Will I be a victim of an attack?' or 'If Nanny has died and then you and Mum die, what will happen to me?'

Reassurance is what they're looking for here. Letting them know that they're safe, that you're there for them, and encouraging them to tell you about their concerns is the best you can do.

What does 'we can't afford it' mean?

Those lovely people in the world of marketing have a knack at pitching toys, trainers, mobile phones, widescreen TVs and many other consumer desirables and high-priced luxury items at those with the spending power (adults) via those with the pester power (children). From an early age kids can be manipulated to crave the coolest gadgets. They get envious of their peers and parents can feel pressured to keep up with the junior Joneses. But no matter how much you may want your kid to have the latest gear, is it worth getting yourself into mountains of debt over? Instead, give your child a better grounding in life by saying 'no' a few times. It may not be easy for them to grasp why their friend has something that they don't and the response of 'we can't afford it' can trigger a new line of questioning. Some dads elaborate by explaining that the money they earn is paying for things like your child's home (and their bedroom full of toys), dinner and the family pets, etc. It's a simple lesson in the value of money and helps your kid realise that new things come at a cost. Alternatively, if they really want something then introduce the idea of saving pocket money for it – giving them a crash course in budgeting in the process. By the time they've saved enough for whatever fad toy they fancy, the chances are they have moved on to another object of desire.

Why do I have to go to school?

In the UK the failure to ensure your child receives an education or attends the school they're registered at can lead to prosecution for parents. OK, that's a huge guilt trip to hang on your five-year-old's shoulders when they decide to throw a sickie. Instead, point out that all children need to go to school to learn useful things, then try challenging them to a race to get ready – that can be enough to shift their mindset out of the 'don't want to go' mode. This works if it's early in their school life and their reluctance stems from that fact that they're missing being at home (with you or mum) or just prefer playing with their toys than having to do any hard work like 'learning stuff'.

Try accentuating the positive too, 'Come on, get ready for school – you've got to meet your friends.' (It helps if you know their friends' names at this point too.) If you find there are more regular meltdowns occurring in the morning then there may be something happening at school that requires further investigation. Take the time to ask your child what has happened that's putting them off school. Often, it'll involve friendships – so a quick lesson in finding other friends to play with may do the trick. Don't be afraid to raise it with their teacher too – asking them about your child's behaviour in class, who they play with or anything that may be making them unhappy.

Milestone 60

Picking pocket money
Age: five onwards

How much pocket money you give to your child and when you start doing so is dependent on the family budget of course – and what they're expected to spend it on. Is it for sweets and treats while you pay for things like trips to the cinema and theme parks?

There are no rules on how much to give or when, but you might want to think about how you give it and what your kids can learn about money in the process. Generally, the sooner they're familiar with coins and notes, the quicker they begin to appreciate the value of money. By the age of seven, kids' money habits have started forming – ideas around saving for what they might like to buy are taking shape. Even if it's just to acknowledge their growing independence, giving some form of pocket money is a good platform for learning – they will make mistakes, but they'll learn from those errors.

Ballpark figures
A recent survey by the UK Halifax Building Society found that the average pocket money per week given to kids aged 5–14 is £7.04 ($8.50) but that varies by region, too. In the more 'affluent areas' like Greater London the figure was 10 per cent above the average, whereas in less affluent ones it was around 5 per cent lower than average.

Gender divide
Conducting a survey into pocket money is a great way for a bank or financial firm to get some coverage in the press, as the Money Advice Service found with their 'CHILDWISE Monitor Report'. That study found that girls aged between 5 and 16 receive 20 per cent less pocket money on average a week than boys of the same age.

Rewarding experience

Where possible, parents use pocket money as an incentive to get their children to do chores and so learn valuable lessons about work ethics, saving and the value of money. Since only one in four kids receive money management advice of any kind in school (thanks again, Money Advice Service for this figure), Dad's role as banker and financial adviser could come in handy.

Changing times

These days, pocket money doesn't have to come in cash bundles – pocket money cards and apps are increasingly being used by parents as a more secure way of doling out the dosh and even monitoring spending.

Dad's tales: Job's worth

'My sons get £4 ($4.85) each for cleaning the car, a couple of quid for mowing the lawn and sweeping the garden. They've both had a weekly amount over the years but the deal is that they clean out their pets and vacuum their room in return for it. '

Paul, father of Jake and Seb

Milestone 61

Your kid makes the school team

Age: eight onwards

Football, netball, hockey, swimming, tag rugby, school debating – whichever minor gathering of enthusiastic youngsters turned out in the same kit they make it on to, you have every right to treat the moment they first get picked as being on par with making the national team for a World Cup Final. Not only are you celebrating the symbol of achievement that comes with being selected – yeah, even as the goalie – you're also proud that they've been accepted into the fold. They're experiencing that landmark moment when the door opens to all that being on a 'team' entails – the bonding, building and co-operative bullshit that starts now and will carry on until at least the time your child retires from work or drops down dead because of it.

In the meantime celebrate what 'being on the team' means for them or see how to give them fatherly support if they don't make the cut.

Pros of being on a team
- It'll build confidence. They'll learn their strengths, work on their weaknesses and gain greater self-awareness.
- It teaches lessons. Kids gain experience of winning and losing and that things won't always go their way. They develop bonds in defeat as well as success.
- It helps with communication. Kids on school teams come into more regular contact with kids from other schools and adults, including coaches and referees, who aren't their friends. It helps them develop social skills and combats shyness.

And if they don't make the cut

- Avoid the blame game. Saying stuff like 'the sports teacher is a muppet' may seem like the best response to help heal your kid's sense of rejection but it won't help their motivation and may just make them angrier.
- Open up their options. Sometimes just saying 'never mind, you'll get in next time' can be enough to help them realise it's not the end of the world and even give them the confidence to give it another shot.
- Offer alternatives. If not making the team means that they're now free on Saturday mornings, offer them a treat, a trip somewhere or a suggestion of something else they'd enjoy using that time for. For dads who often want to provide a fix or actionable solution this might particularly appeal. Learn something about your kid's character from the way they react to this. Kids are pretty resilient and move on quickly.

DAD FACTS: Team spirit

A survey of more than 14,000 teenagers found that those who participated in team sports were less likely to use drugs, smoke, have under-age sex, carry weapons or have unhealthy eating habits.
Archives of Pediatric and Adolescent Medicine

Milestone 62

Civil war among siblings
Age: four onwards

When there's more than one child in the family there's always the potential for some angst that can make added demands on your role as peacekeeper, disciplinarian, fun dad, etc. There are plenty of reasons not to just sit back and 'let 'em battle it out' – including the possibility that one of them really will hurt the other.

Symptoms of sibling rivalry sound like this:

'Daddy! Daddy! he/she ...

... keeps calling me names'

... keeps taking my things'

... keeps telling tales on me'

The reasons why your offspring are bickering can range from being a means of trying to get their parents' attention, to a sense of their sibling being seen as the 'favoured one', or them just being bored or aggressive. While their infighting might indirectly teach them a few life skills to do with arguing, power struggles and conflict resolution, none of this will seem worth it when they're going at it hammer and tongs while you are trying to work from home, are on the phone or are just trying to haul them around the supermarket.

Which kids are most likely to fight?

Sibling dynamic	Likelihood of conflict
Both kids feel they're treated equally	25/1
Same gender: brother on brother/sister on sister	5/1

Sibling dynamic	Likelihood of conflict
Age gap of three years or less	4/1
Toddler and new baby (toddlers can resent the new baby for taking up so much of your time while not being big enough for them to play with)	3/1
Identical twins (all that comparison and contrast only goes to fan the flames of stiff competition)	odds-on

How to handle rival siblings

First, accept that siblings will fight – and that it may not be as bad you think it is. Australian researchers found that parents rate the quality of sibling relationships differently from how the children themselves rate them. It turns out that a child's opinion of their relationship with a sibling is more optimistic than a parent's view.

However, when all else fails:

- Split them up. We're not talking adoption here – just separate them when they're fighting or teasing one another. The realisation that by walking away one of them can diffuse the situation themselves will sink in ... by the time they're about 25.
- Give older children privileges as well as responsibilities. Some experts suggest rewarding the older sibling for modelling good behaviour to the younger one(s) as a means of ramming this home.
- Come up with a list of basic rules that everyone has to adhere to – regardless of age – in a bid to create some 'fairness' in the family (e.g. 'no hitting').
- Always avoid asking 'who started it?' as at some point you'll be told that you did by having more than one child ...

Milestone 63

Your kid's first phone
Age: 10 years ... if you're lucky

It's a moment of separation that, if you can, you should put off for as long as possible. Once the phone is in their hands you have to lay down a whole new set of rules just to get their attention. It becomes a tool for division, a weapon for punishment – but an easy way to get hold of your kid when they're out of your sightline.

The average age a child gets their first smartphone is 10. It's an almost inevitable parent purchase and it pays to get some advice on what to buy and how to manage it. I lost my battle in this war long ago, but Matthew Moreton, managing director at Compare and Recycle, has a few useful tips when choosing a phone for your kid:

- Consider budget, durability, what repair costs might be and data allowance.
- Get familiar with what monitoring tools and apps are available.
- Agree the purpose for your child to have a phone. Is it just to keep in touch, safety reasons, entertainment, independence or all of the above?
- Does your child know how the web works (e.g. cyber bullying and the risks involved with sharing information online)?

These talks need to be carried out prior to discussing with your child the possibility of getting a phone. Once you've made them aware (some may say terrified) about the dangers of smartphone ownership, there comes the pointless exercise that is 'setting parameters'.

'Talk about times and places where phones are not allowed, for instance, family dinners, during classes and bedtime,' suggests Moreton. 'Discuss consequences if the rules are violated.' On the plus side, Moreton says there are various iOS or Android apps that link your child's phone to yours and allow you to control installations, downloads and time spent using different functionalities. (On the minus side, you need to be an 11-year-old to know how to set them.) Finally, have review sessions to see how your child is getting on and don't delay conversations if you see phone use affecting your child's performance at school.

Shock-proof purchase

'Manage your expectations,' says Moreton. Their phone is likely to live in a backpack and generally be subject to more rigours in the playground. If you're getting them a high-end phone then fit a case and a screen protector ... and take out insurance (I speak from costly experience on this). Moreton also suggests getting a simple 'dumbphone'. 'They're about as durable as they come'. (Ideal for a scout camp trip perhaps but lacking any street cred to be seen with). 'If you do go for a smartphone, then we'd recommend steering clear of the more expensive flagship devices as not only can these be a target for thieves, but they also tend to be less durable'.

Milestone 64

Dads' race exposes the dad bod

Age: primary years

Over the years, I've interviewed men for various magazines who've been on a journey to retrieve their fitness and get back into shape. Some do it through cycling, joining the gym, taking up running or rediscovering a past passion like football or boxing.

Almost all cite the same reasons for why they got out of shape in the first place:

1. discovered drinking
2. started uni/work so no time for exercise
3. the kids came along.

New dads are at risk of developing the 'dad bod' and a study of more than 10,000 men (published in the *American Journal of Men's Health*) revealed that new dads gain an average of 2kg (4.4lb) after becoming a dad for the first time. Non-fathers of the same age examined in the same survey were found on average to lose 0.6kg (1.4lb) during the same time frame. The impact a child has upon your time – which you may previously have devoted to exercise – your energy levels, sleep patterns, finances and even your diet – can all affect your health and your waistline. If you want to return to slender or just keep tabs on any flab after you become a dad, you need to take steps.

Dave Hunter, personal trainer and founder of Hunter Movement, suggests the following ways to stay fit for fatherhood:

- Devote dad time. 'The hardest thing for new dads is finding the time. Going off to the gym may not always be possible so that's why it's really important to be able to squeeze things in when you can. Having distance or home programmes to follow is a great way to keep on track and know you're getting a solid workout in, even when time is short.'

- Build a routine. 'Just as you build a routine for your child so you should for your training,' suggests Hunter. 'Try to do small things every day, it's better than one big workout once a week. There is no one-size-fits-all – it's about finding small things that can be implemented constantly and sustainably.'
- Get a goal. 'Running a 10k for a children's charity or just setting yourself a target weight gives you motivation to stick to training. Use your fitness to not only be able to keep and stay active with your kids, but also to be a positive role model and inspiration for them to achieve things, whether it's fitness related or not.'
- Think food. 'Calories in versus calories out is the main thing to consider when trying to lose any excess weight. Increasing your protein intake will help keep you fuller for longer as well as support muscle repair after your workouts.'
- Don't clear their plate. 'Finishing up food kids won't eat is a common cause of calorie intake in "waste not, want not"-citing dads.'

DAD FACTS: Fatherhood – the best medicine

A 2019 survey by private health firm BUPA found that fatherhood is the trigger for 56 per cent of men to take action about their health. In a survey of 100 men with children aged five and under, researchers found that over a third had booked a health assessment after becoming a dad.

Milestone 65

Summer holiday survival
Age: 5–16

It's unlikely that you'll have six solid weeks or more off work too when your kids' school holidays commence, but you'll probably find yourself allocating a chunk of time with them to yourself and your partner as well as grandparents or childminders.

While holidays can be a challenge and you may find yourself counting down the days until they return to school (like a prison inmate eyeing up his release date), they're also a great opportunity to build lasting memories on holidays at home or away. Be prepared to throw some money at some of the summer activities you want to do – though you can cut back the cost of days out by taking your own snacks, booking discount train tickets and parking, or paying for family entrance costs in advance.

If you *were* to take all 30 weekdays of the six-week holiday off work and spend them with your kids, here's how it could – weather permitting – fly by with barely a gadget or digital accessory in sight ...

1. Go for a bike ride.
2. Find a funfair.
3. Take a picnic to the park.
4. Do a day at the theme park.
5. Find a free museum.
6. Go for a campout.
7. See what's on at the cinema.
8. Meet friends for an ice cream.
9. Spend a day at the seaside.
10. Make fruit kebabs and mocktails.

11. Have a treasure hunt.
12. Make and paint at home.
13. Visit a farm.
14. Build a den.
15. Find a local festival.
16. Host a pizza party.
17. Go for a swim.
18. Take a train ride.
19. Hit the water park.
20. Create a puppet show.
21. Have a water fight.
22. Make an indoor obstacle course.
23. Take a walk in the country.
24. Play cricket in a park.
25. Get lost in a library.
26. Have a hide-and-seek marathon.
27. Fly a kite in the park.
28. Head off to the zoo or animal sanctuary.
29. Try out a trampoline.
30. Break out the board games.

Milestone 66

Dealing with the school bully

Age: six onwards

It's a feeling that can turn your stomach over, discovering that your little one is being bullied. They may tell you outright or you may detect the symptoms when they're away from school or the sports club where the bullying may be taking place.

The signs of bullying include a sudden loss of interest in school, taking a different route to and from school, becoming anxious on Sunday evenings, or developing a rash of illnesses – but ones that don't have visible symptoms, such as headaches and stomach pains. Other signs include having nightmares, coming home with bruises, torn clothing or 'lost' personal items, and even bullying others, including siblings.

Before you go storming off to give the other kid's dad a pasting or boot open the school doors like a Wild West cowboy and demand the head teacher's head on a plate, take a deep breath and make the situation a whole lot better for your child by doing the following ...

Look up the school's policy on bullying

It should be on the school website. To get the school onside and to take your concerns seriously, follow the policy to the letter. This usually means making an appointment to see your child's teacher first.

Get the facts straight

'Bullying' is a much misused term. Kids fight, tease and upset one another all the time. Often, they're friends again the next day. But if your child is suffering persistent emotional or physical harm keep a record of when they report it and exactly what they tell you.

Build a defence

Some advisers suggest coaching your child on how to look, walk and talk like a confident person – using non-verbal cues like eye contact, facial expressions and posture to exude confidence and so deflect teasing. Alternatively, joining a father/child self-defence group can give you both a shared interest, keep you both fit and active and help develop self-confidence further.

Put your child first

Avoid the urge to confront the bully's parents. Where you can, let the school deal with it – you never know what is going on in a child's home life, or how the parents will respond. Make sure your child isn't afraid to tell you what's happening – let them know that they don't deserve what's happening to them and it's not their fault.

And what to do if your kid's the bully...

If you're told that your child is making another's hell talk to them about what bullying is, find out why he or she may be doing it and help them understand what their behaviour feels like to others. You may want to monitor what they're doing online or on their phone and talk to the school or club where it's happening about mentoring and bullying awareness. In older children, a behaviour contract or counselling may be needed to put a stop to the torment.

Milestone 67

Parents' evening and feigning an interest in your kid's education

Age: seven onwards

Busy parents can feel guilty that they're not up to speed with what their kid is learning, and it's often only at parents' evenings that issues around their education, behaviour, achievements or struggles suddenly come to light.

According to a 2019 study of more than 2000 parents entitled 'Dumbs and Dads' the majority of fathers don't understand education terminology and nearly half (47 per cent) say they can't make head nor tail of their child's school report. Admittedly, the language of a school report is in itself a lesson in code breaking but the involvement of fathers especially in their children's school life is a matter of increasingly great importance.

According to Charlotte Gater, head of curriculum at Explore Learning, busy lives mean that getting into school is not always possible – but there are some alternative ways of getting involved with your child's learning:

- Can't make parents' evening? 'Ask your partner to record the conversation, prepare some questions ahead of time or ask if the teacher is happy for you to Skype/FaceTime into the meeting.'
- Can you come in to school? 'Do you have a skill that could benefit your child's school? Could you give up a lunch break to run a coding club, give a talk about your occupation or listen to readers before school starts? Schools often run friendly, supportive information sessions on teaching methods, so go along and learn something new.'

- Can you get online? 'Schools' websites have lots of information on the curriculum and teaching methods so use this to be more informed.' Use sites like oxfordowl.co.uk, theschoolrun.com, gov.uk and explorelearning.co.uk/blog for information, resources and advice.
- Can you ask your kid? 'Ask your child good questions about their day. Who hasn't experienced asking a child "How was your day?" and getting the "fine" response? By asking questions that encourage them to give better answers you can engage more meaningful conversations. Try some of these: "What was your maths/English/music class about today?"; "How did you contribute to the class today?"; "What did you enjoy the most about school today?"; "Was anything challenging today?"; "Can you teach me something you've learnt today so I know how to do it too?"'

Bewildered parents who don't understand a method or topic their child is learning can contact their teacher, speak to a tutor or try looking at online help such as BBC Bitesize, where there are lots of great videos explaining different topics. Watch them with your child so you can learn together.

145

Milestone 68

Child gets a bad school report
Age: 10 onwards

Parents' evening usually comes on the back of a school report. A parent's reaction to their child receiving a bad school report can vary from mild disappointment to outright rage depending on their expectations of their child, their own experiences of schooling or the expense paid out to get that private maths tutor. It's little wonder that, back in the day, kids would hide reports or doctor them – taking more care over changing a D to a B on a handwritten report than any of the topics they were studying that year. These days it's virtually impossible to forge a report – short of hacking into the school's mainframe – so kids must face the music/geography/physics.

When your child gets poor grades, doesn't achieve what's been expected or has a few alarming red comments on their report then Kevin Reid, head teacher of Brampton Primary School in East Ham, London, suggests you take the following course of action:

- Don't fly off the handle. 'There may be a whole bunch of reasons why your child isn't achieving/behaving as well as you would like.'
- Do read it through. 'At least twice and pick out the positives. What is your child good at? What have been the successes? Use these to start a conversation about their learning and school. "It says here you're a talented artist ..." (Comedian, if a teacher dared to put that). "Tell me what you like about art?"'
- Don't forget what was said at previous parents' evenings. 'What was your child struggling with and what were their targets? Were there any suggestions given on how to help at home and did you follow through? Again, this isn't a time for reproaching yourself if you hadn't managed to. It will perhaps remind you of where your child

was on their learning trajectory and help you make sense of what the report says now.'

- Do book a time to speak with the class or subject teacher to discuss any concerns you have about the report. 'This should be about next steps in their learning, particular areas they are struggling with and how you can support. Children's learning has to be a partnership between home and school.'
- Don't ignore it. 'If it's suggested that your child doesn't read regularly, try to devise ways you can build it into a regular routine rather than "make" them read for 30 minutes against their will. Take time to visit Waterstones or the local library and choose books that spark an interest. Read together. Children are never too old to be read to and having a good story read to them makes books come to life.'
- Do think about your role if they're getting marked down for being late, absent too often or lacking organisational skills. 'Being punctual, attending regularly and being ready for school are important skills for the future world of higher education and work. What can you do to help? Support your child in preparing the evening before – uniform, school bag, PE kit etc. Encourage going to school even when they are playing up and don't want to. Going to bed a bit earlier and limiting gaming or phone time before bed.'

Be their biggest cheerleader

The most important thing you can do is support. There may be any number of factors that could mean that your child is underachieving. Conditions such as dyslexia or attention disorders in varying forms may only become apparent further into their school life. Raising any concerns you may have with the school's special educational needs (SEN) staff can help in diagnosing any possible issues and getting the best help for your child as soon as possible.

There is plenty of evidence to show that children with interested, supportive parents achieve better on the whole than children whose parents do not appear interested in their child's education. And remember those positives: praise your child for their successes, make a fuss of stickers, certificates and if a teacher tells you anything that is good.

Milestone 69

Exposed to something nasty online

Age: 11 on average

Underage exposure to online pornographic content is one of the biggest fears for UK parents according to one survey of 1500 mums and dads. It found that 75 per cent of parents say their biggest worry is that their children will access – or inadvertently stumble upon – pornography online. It's likely, too. Around 60 per cent of children have used social media by the age of 10, even though many of these have a minimum age requirement of 14. According to some reports, the average age of a child being exposed to porn online is 11 – though others claim that nine is the average.

Although legislation such as the Digital Economy Act, which requires the adult industry to check the age of all online users, is aimed at stopping children seeing harmful content, it's not been enough to keep every child safe. Some schools and groups like the National Society for the Prevention of Cruelty to Children (NSPCC) offer training courses and awareness workshops to advise parents on how to keep their children safe and monitor what they are accessing online. To help prevent your son or daughter from being exposed to unsuitable material or being contacted on social media, but still using the internet, you could look into ...

Managing wi-fi settings

Use your home wi-fi settings to manage what content can be accessed on tablets, phones and computers. See the 'Online Safety' section on the NSPCC website to find out how. In addition, Apple's Screen Time app provides parents with tracking on all the apps that children use across all iOS devices; and Google has a Digital Wellbeing app that shows parents how a phone is used, in addition to Family Link, which helps parents control their children's use of Android.

Putting up blocks

Changing social media settings to disable location tagging and block all but 'friends' can help shield your kids' information. (Some 71 per cent of parents claim they don't know what their children are doing on social media.)

Discussing online dangers

Chat with your kids as soon as you feel they're ready to – or when their school is focusing on e-safety. Talk about their 'digital footprint', how what they post on social media can be used and abused, and the consequences of their images ending up in the wrong hands.

Put it in perspective

Much of the above is practical, well intentioned and most likely only really going to happen in a half-arsed way. Your kid will see some heinous stuff online that children wouldn't have been exposed to before (well not since the days of the plague). You won't be able to manage all they're exposed to, and in that way the internet is really no different from our everyday life. But in the same way, if you can teach your kids what to look out for, what's right and what's not, they will – hopefully – feel they can tell when something is wrong online and stay away or tell you.

13 facts on how dads do things differently

You may not need any convincing of the necessity of your role in raising your child but there are those who don't take dad's influence too seriously – including a few fathers themselves. By way of a little light relief at this stage in the book, here are a few science-backed studies underlining the importance of your role and that what dads do does matter …

Fact 1
A study by the National Institute of Child Health and Human Development (NICHD) shows that dads are more engaged in childcare than ever before, with reasons for this including mothers working more hours and receiving higher salaries and fathers working less.

Fact 2
One US university study found that fathers of daughters sang more, used more language related to the body and to sadness, were more attentively engaged, and used more analytical language. Fathers of sons engaged in more rough-and-tumble play and used more achievement-focused language.

Fact 3
Researchers have documented that mothers spend more time speaking to their children than fathers do. But even if they utter fewer words, it's actually dads who enhance a child's language skills. A 2006 study published in the *Journal of Applied Developmental Psychology* found that the father's vocabulary had a greater impact on the child's language proficiency a year later.

Facts 4-9

Adolescent boys who report having a high-quality, positive relationship with their fathers are:

- less likely to engage in delinquency
- less likely to abuse substances
- less likely to get into trouble in later life.

Adolescent girls who have a close relationship with their fathers are:

- more likely to delay sexual activity
- less likely to become pregnant
- less likely to report experiencing depression.

Fact 10

Boys and girls whose fathers showed more involvement in their lives early on tend to attain higher levels of education. Fathers' engagement was linked to higher academic performance.

Fact 11

Research from the University of Central London suggests that children are more likely to get into trouble in later life if they didn't have 'quality' time, like baths from dad, when they were little 'uns.

Fact 12

Dads have also been shown to spend a higher percentage of their one-to-one interactions with infants in stimulating, playful activity than do mothers – from these interactions, research concludes, children learn how to regulate their feelings and behaviour.

Fact 13

Dads who work out, play sport and generally keep themselves fit and active boost their offspring's brain power. German researchers carrying out trials on mice found that males who exercise prior to mating produce babies with stronger brain neurons, which made them smarter than babies whose dads didn't run on wheels.

The teenager years...

Striving for independence and eager to make their mark in the adult world while going through the stresses of secondary school and the unpredictability of hormones makes this a challenging time for all concerned.

Milestone 70

Kid dresses 'inappropriately'

Age: 10 onwards ... though possibly a lot earlier

Remember, your clothes are much more than just something to wear to keep you warm, trendy and not arrested for indecency. They're a way of communicating, too. Though quite what's being communicated isn't always so easy to determine. It's down to us parents to try to fathom out exactly what they're trying to say – or else to just open up a conversation without making any pre-judgements as to what the motives may be behind the low-slung jeans or Gothic cape, feathered cap and high-heeled boots. This falls under the much-used parenting category of 'going through a phase' and should be treated with kid gloves (preferably not the leather-studded ones your daughter has taken to wearing). Look back on your own teenage years especially and how you may have changed the way you looked to keep up with fashions or fit in with peers, or to communicate one of the following:

- Rebellion. Kids start dressing differently to show that they're individuals; they're buying their own clothes, they've got their own mind and don't want their wardrobe 'controlled' by their parents.
- Attention. It's possible that their choice of dress might be a cry for help. Girls especially who feel pressured into dressing a certain way by peers or social media may choose to dress a certain way to help them cope with feeling unhappy if they feel they can't speak out.
- Belonging. The culture of a particular group of friends your kid starts identifying with could influence the way they're choosing to dress – either because they belong to the group or because they want to.

Talk it over

If you're concerned about how your teenager is dressing, as with any issues to do with behaviour, it usually pays to chat to them about it – but choose your battles and know that you don't have to win every one. Remember that they'll grow out of some things, like fashion fads. But also take an interest. Ask them about the labels they're wearing or the style they're following. They may be reluctant to listen or dismissive of your questions or just not want to engage over how they dress at first but if you take a genuine interest and try to understand where they're coming from it can make discussing what they're wearing – and when you feel they've gone too far – a little easier to raise.

Also, don't assume they're dressing to provoke or generate sexual interest. Girls can be accused of dressing in a 'trashy' or 'tarty' way with the inference that they're looking for sexual compliments and attention. Avoid making judgements on them when they choose to dress differently and instead look to building a relationship that means you're all comfortable talking about their choices without them feeling you're restricting their freedom or independence.

Milestone 71

Having 'a chat'. Serious talk time

Age: phew, there's a quandary ...12?

As you've seen already, parenthood throws up some difficult
but necessary conversations that you must have with your kids
at times, including 'a chat about ...' sex, sexual orientation,
masturbation, alcohol or other drugs, academic difficulties, self-harm,
secrets, theft ... And then there can be your own problems that will
directly affect your children, such as health issues, unemployment,
debt or divorce.

None of these lend themselves to being laugh-a-minute topics
over the family dinner table and every parent is going to have
their own approach. Going through a tricky topic with your
child – from the 'birds and the bees' chat to a discussion about
being gay, having trouble at school or even the repercussions
that unemployment, debt or the breakdown in your relationship
with their mother will have upon them – will not be easy. Avoid
starting serious conversations about these topics just off the cuff.
Trying to broach a subject like money missing from your wallet
or the cuts you've noticed on their arms while you're driving them
to school or when one of you is just about to leave the house isn't
great timing. Instead:

- Pick a moment when you can both chat things through – and hear
  each other out.
- Let them know in advance what you want to talk about – and make
  sure you've had a good think about what you want to say yourself,
  too.

- Chat with your partner about it if that's possible and get each other's thoughts on the issue you want to raise with your child.
- Don't start a conversation with your kid that could get fraught on the back of drinking alcohol.
- Aim to stay calm even when you're shocked by the topic or their reaction to it.
- Don't expect to solve anything in one conversation. Just opening up the chat so that you both feel comfortable talking about it further down the line is a great start. Talking things through – without any expectation of being able to 'fix' things immediately – is enough.

Seek support
Get some perspective. Don't try to deal with delicate family issues on your own. There are support services for parents and counselling groups for families affected by issues such as drug abuse. Talking things through with another adult – especially one trained in listening and offering sound advice from somewhere else other than the bar of the local – can help you to make a breakthrough when you're struggling to get a conversation started with your kid.

Milestone 72

Kid starts coming home late

Age: 13 onwards

How you deal with this moment can have repercussions for years to come. It can be one of the first big challenges to your authority as a parent. It's a major boundary push on your kid's part and possibly not eased by the fact that you've been anxious and are now annoyed at your kid in equal measure. A straw poll of parents I cobbled together via a parenting Whatsapp and social media shout-out revealed that average curfew times for kids aged 13–15 on non-school nights were any time from 7 p.m. to 10.30 p.m. depending on where they supposedly are and if they're being collected.

Curfews seem to work best when you give them a bit of structure – and specifically outline the consequences of what will happen if they're not adhered to. To help teenagers to manage their time-keeping and ease your anxiety, use ploys that have been tried and tested by parents on kids who've learned the hard way when it's time to be home. Some of the rules parents put in place include:

- Homework comes first. Any school stuff is done before they go out and when it's exam time they're home earlier and in bed earlier to get sufficient sleep. If you suspect that fatigue is affecting their school work then consider cutting back on 'going out' time until you see an improvement.
- Check-in times. They have to make a quick call or send a text so you know where she or he is and so that they know what time they're expected home.

- Parent calls. If your kid is hanging out at a friend's house and especially if they're staying over then get a contact name and number for the friend's parents to confirm they're happy with your child being there. (And that the kids are where they say they are.)
- Traffic updates. If your kid is delayed because of traffic or the concert overran or they missed the bus, you expect him or her to follow the check-in rule.
- Number share. Share a phone number with one of your kid's friends. This means that your child has a back-up if their own phone fails, and there is no excuse not to check in.

Repercussions if curfew is broken

If your child arrives home late and you're not satisfied that they've got a justifiable reason for doing so don't be tempted to read them the riot act at 10.35 p.m. on a school night. Point out that you've been worried about them – and you're relieved that they're home OK. The next day is the time to inform them that they've got to earn back the privilege of going out – either with a grounding or a more measured approach whereby you bring forward the curfew time to, for example, 8 p.m. Make it clear that if they stick to the new earlier time and show that they can be responsible then you'll reconsider making it later.

Milestone 73

Issues around body image

Age: 12 onwards

Insecurity and anxiety around body image can come to the fore in teens, especially for girls, as many of them focus so much of their energy, effort and cash on their appearance. While it has troubled teens for generations, the rise of social media has taken image consciousness to another stratosphere. Being tagged in a photo on Instagram while not looking your best is – according to one study by Common Sense Media – the worst worry in life for 35 per cent of all teenage girls. (The same study found that over a fifth of them feel bad about themselves when nobody comments on or 'likes' the photos they post.)

The horse has long since bolted when it comes to reigning in social media's influence on teenagers and image, but as a dad you still have a huge part to play in helping your little girl or boy through these troubled times. Psychologists will point out how dads have a major impact on their daughters' view of men and how they feel about themselves. How you talk about women, appearance and issues such as weight can influence your daughter's feelings about herself. When tiptoeing around the subject of 'looks' it's worth noting the following:

- Do – keep the father–daughter relationship close while they're growing up since research shows that girls are more likely to have self-confidence and good levels of assertiveness if their dads have made a conscious effort to spend one-on-one time with them.
- Don't – put huge value on looks, even if it's just comments about celebrity females, when you're around your daughter. It can send out messages to her still-developing mind that looks matter more than intellect, achievements or kindness.

- Do – show her that you respect and admire women as complete individuals – sing the praises of the qualities, strengths and abilities you see in women you know when you're with your daughter.
- Don't – criticise her appearance, weight or shape. Even in jest. Whether she's overtly conscious of how her body is changing or not, she really won't want or need that kind of thing from her dad. Of course compliment her on what she's wearing or the way she's changed her hair. Just be conscious of how sensitive she may be about her looks and physical changes.
- Don't – forget to praise her strengths – generosity, sense of humour, academic skills, etc. – all the things that make her unique. Be the role model who places value on her many positive attributes aside from her looks.

Of course, this is all about tips for dads of daughters but that's not to say teenage sons don't suffer the same anxieties around body image, the same self-consciousness as their body grows and the same worries about how they're viewed by peers, parents and everyone. Indeed the insecurities around body image can be even tougher for boys to confront and deal with because of our tendency, as chaps, to bottle things up and suffer in silence. Apply these guidelines to your child whatever their gender and ensure that no matter what the outside world may do to upset them that you've always got their back.

Milestone 74

Putting it all down to hormones

Age: 13 onwards

If you've found fatherhood has been a journey that involves staggering from one family crisis to another from pretty much the moment your firstborn appeared then the latest teenage eruptions won't come as too much of a surprise. Although nurture will no doubt account for some of the issues you may find yourself having with your teenage son or daughter, nature plays a big part, too. Although puberty and hormonal earthquakes are just part of adolescence, which also includes cognitive, social and emotional changes, they really do have a major impact on teenagers in many ways. Here's what they are doing inside your kid ...

Gonadotropin-releasing hormone (GnRH)
This appears on the scene at the beginning of puberty, and is the 'Kevin the Teenager' trigger for teenage boys and girls. Known to its friends as GnRH, it's the catalyst for the release of other hormones that run wild, in turn making your child run wild too.

Follicle-stimulating hormone (FSH)
FSH does what it says on the tin, stimulating the growth of follicles and causes a werewolf-like effect on the unsuspecting child.

Luteinising hormone (LH)
LH combined with FSH in girls instructs the ovaries to begin producing oestrogen and eggs. In boys, the LH and FSH combo tells the testes to begin producing testosterone (the male sex hormone) and sperm.

Oestrogen, progesterone and testosterone

These are the sex drive hormones that also account for your child's heightened aggression and sudden passion for risk-taking behaviour – stunts, dares, drugs, drink, giving dad a 'load of lip'. Physical changes these hormones kick off include a deeper voice, growing breasts and the start of periods.

Androgens

A spike of these in both boys and girls during puberty causes the skin's oil glands to get larger, make more sebum and bring forth acne.

Melatonin

Another side effect of the GnRH trigger is that it upsets the timing of when melatonin and serotonin (hormones that regulate our sleep cycle) are released. Teenagers become night owls and are a nightmare to wake up in the morning.

A heady cocktail

Together, this cocktail of chemicals can trigger growth spurts, muscle development, spots, hair growth and bodily fluids – and a mix of moods, emotions and psychological reactions that you can't. How you cope and help them deal with these changes will vary from one parent to the next – but at least now you know that it's not personal.

Milestone 75

Dads and teenage misbehaviour

Age: 13 onwards

There's no magic formula to making the teenage years better for the adults or the adolescents. We all muddle through as best we can – learning lessons along the way. What works for one family may not work for others.

Here are some insights from some parents who have been there and done that, or who are living through the process at the moment:

> Pick your battles. You can find that some issues aren't worth going into a full-blown war over. You have to work out what you can give way on – and when you do have a row don't take it personally, a lot of it is down to where your child's at in their life.
>
> **Simon, father of Gus, Finley and Cerys**

> My modus operandi has always been (A) don't sweat the small stuff and (B) when it is no longer small I would use silence and smouldering disappointment to maximum effect. As that famous philosopher R. Keating said "You say it best when you say nothing at all". If the situation warranted the big guns I would raise my voice SO LOUD that my anger was evident but also maximised by the fact that it happened about as often as a Charlton Athletic Wembley appearance.
>
> **Mark, father of Beth and Ellen**

❛ Never try to "win" an argument with a teenager. The moment you adopt that mindset is the moment you lose. Parent–child relationships should not be adversarial – they should be conspiratorial. Define the real issue that's at hand – the real 'enemy' – then work together to surmount it in a way that's mutually satisfying. ❜
Joe, father of Paul and Claire

❛ I've got four boys – two sons, two stepsons – who are between the ages of 12 and 14. Rather than break a scrap up – because that's what they want, adult interaction – I stand and watch with eyes bulging like the referee Pierluigi Collina studying the crimes being committed on the "pitch" in front of me. When they've finished, both are waved over and shown "the red card": they're ordered to bed. As they head to their "dressing room", I'll shout, "I'll see you in half an hour and make sure your piggy banks are ready." We then enter "the courtroom". I'll ask, "What went on there, then?" "He did this, he did that," etc., etc. I'll listen, remind them of the space limitations in the flat then hand out the punishment. "You £5, you £5 – and remember it's going towards your school uniform next year. Now get in there and apologise to your mother/stepmother." So far most of their secondary school uniforms and PE kit have come from household crimes. The trick is to be consistent. Crimes are few and far between nowadays – they can't afford otherwise. ❜
Lee, father of two sons and two stepsons

❛ 'Accept that a lot of what upsets your kids is often nothing to do with Mum or Dad – it's not our fault. They've had a bad day at school or a falling out with a friend or boyfriend or they've seen or heard something that's annoyed them. It can escalate quite often at home – but the root cause, I've often later discovered, isn't anything we've done. ❜
Tom, father of Kate and Thomas

Milestone 76

Kid is struggling at school
Age: 13 onwards

Exam season is often the first time you witness your kids suffering the pressure that comes with delivering to a deadline. In that way it's a passable preparation for the world of work – though arguably it has little else in common with adult life.

In order to prepare kids for the unnatural stress of exams numerous governments have over the years devised tests for kids – like SATS – that seem to start not long after they've learned to walk. Because of this, the signs of stress that follow may be noticeable in your child long before they're sitting down in a secondary school exam hall.

Schools do offer support and advice for pupils who are struggling with the pressures of exams, but it's more likely that the people who know their kids the best (that's you) will see the signs of stress first. If you don't, then here's a cheat's guide to identifying exam stress early:

- Sleep disturbances. Sleepness nights, especially for teens, that aren't related to bingeing on Netflix can be a result of issues at school
- Off their food. Skipped meals and picking at the food on their plate are symptoms of stress. OK, it can be hard to determine if this is exam-related or just normal behaviour, but sudden changes in your child's eating patterns at any time can often be a sign of other issues beyond a disliking for the new cereal.
- Low mood. A sign that they're not coping well with the demands of school work, revision and the pressure of exams.
- Low confidence. Being asked to recall nuggets of information on a dozen different subjects from several years of study at a specific time in the space of a couple of weeks is bound to knock their self-esteem.

- Frustration. We've all been there. It happens when the juggling act gets too manic and you tend to snap at those closest to you.
- Physical flare-ups. Upset stomach, headache, migraine, hay fever and eczema – these are all more likely to flare up at exam time partly in response to the stress.

How you can help

Amy Przeworski, an associate professor in the Clinical Division of the Department of Psychological Sciences at Case Western Reserve University, specialises in anxiety and stress in children. She says parents can play a major part in helping their children cope with stress in general and especially at exam time in a number of ways, including ...

Starting the conversation

'You seem like you are stressed.' Or, if you don't know if your child is stressed, you can ask by saying something like 'Are you stressed out right now?' 'Encourage them to express their feelings using their words. When they do, validate it by saying things like "I can understand how that would stress you out. That would stress anyone out." As with adults, just getting the words out and acknowledging how they're being affected by whatever's troubling them can be the key to getting something off your chest and dealing with it.'

Seeking the solution

'When problem solving, you want the child to generate solutions – go through the list of possible solutions and together with your child identify which ones seem like the best options,' says Przeworski. 'Allow your child to choose one or two that seem like the best options. This does not mean that you do not have any input as a parent. You can rule out solutions that simply won't work – like "Dad I'm struggling with maths, will you do it for me?"'

Keeping calm

'Kids resonate with their parents emotions,' says Przeworski. It may be that you as a parent getting stressed out about the exams will increase any stress that they are experiencing. 'If your child is feeling stressed or anxious, note your own level of stress or anxiety and instead try to do stress reducers with your kids. For example, I do yoga with my kids. Or I may take a walk with them in the sunshine. Sometimes we have dance parties. All of these things help me and my kids to relieve stress together, which makes for a happier and calmer home environment.'

Bunking off school

Teachers go to great pains to point out the link between high attendance and high achievement at school, but not every kid gets the message. For various reasons – including bullying, struggling academically, bad relationships with teachers, peer pressures, issues at home or disengagement with the school in general – some students will start playing truant. In some cases – around 5 per cent of UK students – it becomes a habit. That's not only disruptive to their education but also puts them at risk of being excluded. What's more, as their parent you could be fined and taken to court, and that's not to mention the strain the situation could put on you as a family.

So, how do you deal with it if the school tells you your child has been truanting? Here are a few strategies:

- Ask your child why. Are any of the reasons mentioned above a factor? Or is it something else. They may give you a different explanation to the one they gave to their teacher. Getting to the root cause of the problem is vital, and you need to tackle it as soon as you're aware it exists – the longer anxiety about school persists, the deeper it becomes.
- Talk to the school. They'll probably contact you anyway but be proactive and seek to work with the staff to support your child. Find out what options the school offers for dealing with the issues your child has with the school. It's in the best interests of the school to get your child's attendance back on track.
- Drive it home. Be prepared to sacrifice some time and effort to ensuring your child keeps up their side of any 'contract' you may have with the school. You may need to get your workplace on board – giving you the flexibility to take your child into school.
- Do your homework. Get familiar with your child's school policy on dealing with issues such as bullying if that's a reason for the truanting. If you're unhappy with the way the school responds to your concerns, escalate to the school leader or the school governors, the Local Education Authority (LEA) or the Academy Trust.

Milestone 77

Kid comes home drunk
Age: 13 onwards

Hangovers are scientifically proven to get worse the older you get –
and that's especially true for parents of teenagers with a hangover.
At times, your average teen can be contrary, argumentative and even
aggressive – almost acting as if they're drunk. Now imagine what it's
like when they actually are. When your teen comes home intoxicated
it's normal for even the most liberal of parents to feel a tinge of
disappointment. But most of us just hit the roof.

Of course, the heat of the moment is not the ideal time to overreact.
You need to wait until the cold light of day to do that. As a parent, you
need to manage the drunkenness situation first – be firm, decisive and
fair. Get them to bed – ensuring they have water and a bucket. Check
on them in the night. Then start the inquest the next morning. The
reasons for doing this are:

- Waiting until the next morning means your lecture will hold their
  attention and have added resonance when they're 'absolutely
  hangin'.
- You'll get more accurate responses to questions such as 'where did
  you get the alcohol from?'
- You're more likely to be able to try to find out what's led to this
  incident – it might not be a stage they're going through. Could
  there be a habit forming here? Explain your concerns, the risks
  involved and get them to understand where you're coming from.
- You can then reassure them that whatever happens, you're their
  dad, you'll always be there for them and that you're quite partial to
  a New Zealand pinot if they're ever looking for a drinking partner.

Milestone 78

First stand-up row with your teenager
Age: 13 onwards

If you didn't wait until the next day to discuss your kid's failure to come home on time and it all kicks off in the front room then fill this in once the dust has settled. Look for themes, common 'blow-up' points and where you could have got a better response in, then refer to this before your next argument with your angry teen.

You: ....

Your teenage child: ....

You: ....

Your teenage child: ....

You: ....

Your teenage child: ....

You: ....

Your teenage child: ....

You: ....

Your teenage child: ....

You: ....

Your teenage child: ....

You: ....

Your teenage child: ....

You: ....

Your teenage child: ....

You: ....

Your teenage child: ....

Door slams.

Milestone 79

Fixing your kid's 'laziness'

Age: 13

When tipping into the teenage years, some young people start to 'reprioritise' their activities and attitudes towards things like household chores, sports, homework and getting out of bed. Partly it's down to the physical changes they're going through (see Milestone 74 – hormones) but sometimes it's a case of picking up bad habits or requiring greater motivation to do stuff (see Milestone 60 – pocket money).

It's not about 'laziness' but more likely a symptom of being frustrated, discouraged, disillusioned, defiant or even lacking in confidence. Sometimes it's about laying out your expectations when it comes to everyday domestic routines – or demonstrating what you expect.

Bedroom case study

So, take bedrooms for instance. On a Saturday morning you notice that their bedroom resembles the aftermath of an earth tremor of around 8 on the Richter scale – and yet there have been no radio or TV reports to suggest that that's the cause of the devastation you're looking at. Here's a three-step guide to getting your kid back into good habits:

1. Give them specifics. What's expected from 'tidy your room'? In their opinion it may be tidy – compared with what it could be. 'Clothes in laundry basket or wardrobe, floor vacuumed, sheets changed.' Give them specifics so that there's no ambiguity. (You may have to demonstrate every now and then the standards you're asking for).

2. Give them some leeway. Give a bit of control back to them by avoiding 'do it NOW!' ultimatums. Opt for a time frame, such as 'by 3 p.m.' They'll probably leave it to the last minute but you'll have given them a chance and you won't have to keep asking them half a dozen times.
3. Give them consequences in advance. 'If it's not done by 3 p.m. you're not going out/watching the film/playing on your phone at 6 p.m.' Deal? To make it stick as a habit you may need to look at rewards and incentives – screen time/pocket money/other privileges.

The teenage clock

Sleep will be critical to your child's physical and emotional well-being as well as helping him or her to build resilience. In their teens, their body clock changes and they're more likely to stay up later and sleep in later. Some schools and colleges are even changing their start times to acknowledge this and get the best out of their students. Getting your child into good sleep habits will help them to cope better with the changes they undergo. Here are the recommended amounts of sleep for children of different ages:

- school-age children (6–13 years old): 9–11 hours
- teenagers (14–17 years old): 8–10 hours
- younger adults (18–25 years old): 7–9 hours.

Milestone 80

First time as the dad taxi
Age: 13 onwards

This role is created for you by wearing you down over time; by doing school runs, driving them to sports clubs or dropping them off at friends' parties they come to have an expectation that – when wheels are required – you are truly an Uber-father. According to a Sainsbury's Bank survey of 2000 parents with kids aged 8–16, it was estimated that 22 days of an adult parent's entire life is devoted to being a taxi service for their kids. It also found that dads and mums who drive clock up one hour and 23 minutes every week sitting in cars to collect their kids from sports activities and hobbies – also devoting an average of 40km (25 miles) a week to these extra-curricular activities.

Here are some ideas to make it all a bit more bearable:

- Taxi tipping. So, tips? Yes, it would nice to get some from your kids wouldn't it? Maybe 10 per cent of their pocket money, allowance or their own earnings could be contributed to the petrol costs. Good luck with that.
- Fare's fair. Opt perhaps for a medieval barter system for services rendered – if they want a lift somewhere on a Saturday night, then their Sunday morning could be spent repaying you with a valet service.

Home James (Bond)

Alternatively, to see what you'll get out of all this try to look at that average 'one hour, 23 minutes' in a different light. For many kids, that journey in the front seat of the 'taxi' with dad is the only time they'll spend alone with you and (relatively) without distraction. And vice versa. Conversations held between father and child while stuck in traffic can help you both discover one another's hopes, dreams, interests and musical tastes. The most common phrase used on these taxi rides are 'Don't tell Mum but ...' See it as a chance to relate, to open up to each other ... and then when they're feeling the bond, ask for a tip.

Milestone 81

Hosting a teenage party
Age: 15 onwards

You've probably already read about teenage parties held at parents' homes while innocently googling terms like 'Facebook' and 'ransacked' but it is possible to be the dad who throws a decent party for a mass of adolescents and lives to tell the tale. Just bear in mind that you're taking responsibility for more than just your own teenager. Clear the house of valuables, warn the neighbours in advance and pin up some ground rules that will help keep the gatecrashers and local constabulary from the door.

Party rules
1. Party-goers by invitation only – if word spreads beyond those invited then THE PARTY'S OFF.
2. Under-18s must obey the laws of the land when it comes to alcohol. If they don't, THE PARTY'S OFF.
3. All guests must obey the laws of the land when it comes to drugs. If they don't, THE PARTY'S OFF.
4. Music is to be played at a volume that won't cause structural damage. If it isn't, THE PARTY'S OFF.

Most of the above will be taken with a pinch of salt by any teenager worthy of the name – they'll also be looking to play as much music as they can that features offensive language, snog, smoke cigarettes and wander into any parts of the house you've deemed 'off limits'.

What to do on the big night
How you manage this is a test in parental tact.
Act as bouncer
Getting your child to police the low-level stuff – while also checking that she and he is OK and not worried about anything or anyone at the party – is one option. Having bouncers on the door is another.

Combining these two ploys – you answer the door to all guests (only have one entrance on the night) and your son/daughter vouches for them – will keep the gatecrashers out.

Play the host

Keep the food coming throughout the evening – it's a valid excuse for you to mingle among the party-goers, checking on the state of the guests and looking out for any potential trouble.

Bring a friend ...

Can you combine the party so it's a joint affair with one of your child's friends? A joint party may mean more guests but also a greater number of parents/responsible adults there to police it.

Keep a clear head

Steer clear of drinking – even though it may seem like the only way to get through hosting a teenage party with your nerves intact; you'll need to be in a sober state to deal with any trouble.

Know the law

In the UK it's against the law for an adult to buy alcohol on behalf of someone under 18 and for someone under 18 to drink alcohol in licensed premises. It is not illegal for a child aged 5–17 to drink alcohol at home or on other private premises. It's your call on this if it's a private party but you may want to talk to the parents of those attending before allowing any alcohol to be drunk.

Know when to call time

When the time comes to call it a night, issue a few last warnings to your child and if needs be call taxis or parents to take kids home. Or have some spare bedding ready for those who need it. Don't let any kids who've been drinking or taking drugs walk home if you can help it.

DAD TALK: Throwing up a party

'When my eldest daughter turned 16 and asked for a party we said "yes, but only your immediate friends and do not get drunk". My tip would be – expect the worst and anything less is a bonus. Also, I would never let any of my kids have a house party if we were not in. All the parties that I went to went wrong when there were no adults to control us.'

Torre, father of Angel, Lily-Ann and Isabella

Milestone 82

Kid caught doing drugs

Age: 15

Lots of teenagers experiment with drugs though only a small proportion of those who do so will develop a problem. Some people, such as Neil Coles, a young person's drug worker with Addaction, a leading UK drug, alcohol and mental health support charity, spend a lot of their time advising parents and schools about how to have informed conversations with young people about drug and substance use. He suggests that parents ...

Keep calm
'Many parents feel lost and confused when they find out their young person is using drugs. This can lead to fear driving their reaction.' Coles says that disciplinary responses – such as confiscating phones or stopping them seeing particular friends – may feel protective, but can only serve to drive a wedge between parent and child. 'Young people will experiment, push boundaries, and take risks. The majority won't develop serious issues or become dependent – don't panic and try not to allow conversations to become arguments by asking open questions that encourage them to talk.'

Do your homework
'Parents often report to me that the gulf between them and their young person seems unbridgeable.' Coles says that parents need to be learning about the types of substances young people may use, why they experiment, and their effects. 'You don't need to be an expert but feeling a bit more confident in your knowledge about drugs and alcohol will help you.'

Keep it real

Using threats like 'that stuff will kill you' can actually be counterproductive. 'Feeding them wrong information can undermine your advice. Make them aware of the information you've found and where they may be able to get the support they need,' says Coles.

Ask around

Support services like Addaction run Parent Partnership programmes to help parents find supportive ways of dealing with a drug or drink issue. This specialist support is worth reaching out to when you discover your child is using drugs – and you can do so anonymously.

Kid gets in trouble with the police (*Age: 10 onwards*)

Often the first you learn of your son or daughter's run-in with the law will be when the police contact you by phone or appear on your doorstep. You'll be understandably upset, disappointed, angry, mortified – or all of the above. Depending on the severity of the misdemeanour and the local laws of the land your child could be facing a warning, a curfew order or a court summons. Whatever happens further down the line, when you're first made aware that the police want to speak to you about what your child has been up to remember to ...

Take five

Avoid making a bad situation worse by losing your temper. Aim to find out as much as possible about what the police say your kid has done.

Ask all

Talk to your child as soon as possible, in private. Give them time to reply and explain.

Take advice

In the event of your child being charged or facing further criminal proceedings, seek legal advice from a professional legal representative who's well versed in youth criminal matters.

Milestone 83

Giving them careers advice

Age: 12 onwards

At around the age of 12 your daughter will announce that her hard-held ambition is to become a beauty blogger. Alternatively, your son will respond to any careers-related question with the answer 'anti-terrorist tactical response vehicle driver' (or else he'll want the blog job and she's yearning for the anti-terror vocation).

As much as you admire their sense of social responsibility or desire to provide a running commentary on the application of lip gloss to camera for hours on end in lieu of rent, you will have to take on the role of informal careers adviser and arm them with a few harsh facts about working life. One survey, from www.notgoingtouni.com, revealed that a quarter of teenagers have no idea what to do after they leave compulsory education. You could just sow a few seeds about the thought of future careers, apprenticeships or further education if you:

- Talk to them from time to time about possible careers they might be interested in and why they appeal. Don't make a big deal out of it – because they'll have changed their mind by teatime – but chats about what you do might start a chat about what *they'd* like to do.
- Encourage them to talk to other grown-ups in the family and your network of friends, asking about different career experiences – nurture the idea of having work contacts, networking and nepotism.
- Help them to explore possible employers, apprenticeship providers or further education courses on offer in your local area – don't do the work for them, but when the time's right, offer to read applications or help find firms that fit the bill of what your child wants to get into.

- Keep an eye out for things like open days (at colleges and training organisations) and careers fairs held locally.
- Find out when your child's school will put on careers events, parents' evening with careers advisers or job fairs, as well as the 'work experience' programmes that are commonly run during Key Stage 4 or in the sixth form.

Take them to work

If you're from the old school of 'grafting since you could walk' you'll have instilled a work ethic in your kids and nurtured their business acumen from the moment they could master eBay. The next step will be exposing them to the horrors of commuting, office politics and contributing to the staff collections via a 'take your kid to work' day. However, it's much more likely that you'll need to give them a bit more signposting as they progress through their teens.

Milestone 84

Having to punish your teenager
Age: 13 onwards

Adolescents are hormonally wired to kick off at the slightest perception of injustice. Dealing with troubled teens is a topic that's filled countless books and provided the plot line to a fair few films too. There is no perfect solution. Instead, you could opt for a dad's conflict resolution plan – one that might curtail the behaviour you don't approve of without leading to a major meltdown.

Don't...

Lose your temper – easier said than done of course but the experts in these matters say that you just make 'losing it' become an acceptable way of dealing with issues in relationships.

Break your own rules – aim to be consistent in your punishment. Set the boundaries, remind them of the rules and if they break them, make the punishment appropriate. Look out for being played off against your partner or the pair of you not being consistent or united about a disciplinary issue.

Give them a guilt trip – teens especially don't react well to a parent who uses guilt as a punishment. Some parents will hit them with 'no wonder I'm always angry/tired/broke it's because of you! ...' This tends to have the effect of distancing them, or forcing outside problems on to them, which they're not yet mature enough to deal with.

Lecture them – for starters, you're wasting your time. Their attention span is all over the show at this age and they'll have switched off in seconds. You're better off asking them to explain the reasons why they've not done their school project, been rude to people, hit the head teacher and so on instead of giving them a 10-minute rant on the importance of education, making the right choices or what 'my dad used to do to me ...'

Compare with siblings – No parent who grew up with siblings should need reminding of how divisive and demeaning the moan that 'your sister/brother never does this' can be. It just breeds resentment.

Do...

Prepare them for punishment – 'You've left your room untidy – right, that's it, no TV/tablet/phone for tonight.' Random punishments that curtail their favourite pasttime might seem like the best way for your kid to learn harsh lessons but they don't have a longer-term effect on changing behaviour. Try negotiating the consequences of any misdemeanours in advance so that lessons are learned. For example, if they come home late, they have to be home early until they've regained your trust. The untidy bedroom could mean a reduction in pocket money for chores not done.

Milestone 85

Parental differences
Age: 13 onwards

Emotions, hormones, stress of work and school, peer pressure, family history, relationship dynamics, teenage angst, parental frustration – whatever the reasons, the teenage years can be among the toughest times for families. Often, the tension in the household can contribute to the breakdown in family relationships temporarily or for years and years. Research shows that divorce risks increase with children's ages – until they reach adulthood – and, statistically, the separation or divorce of parents when their children are in their early teens leaves the most lasting negative impact. A study of more than 6000 British children found that kids whose parents separated during their teens have a 16 per cent greater risk of suffering emotional problems, anxiety and depressive symptoms when compared with infant children.

It's grim reading but of course it's not to say that 'staying together for the sake of the kids' is always the ideal solution. As another survey carried out by family law organisation Resolution found, 82 per cent of teens who had experienced divorce said they preferred their parents to go their separate ways if they are unhappy.

Words of wisdom
Couples going through separation and divorce are advised to talk to lawyers – especially when there are children involved – but before getting to the stage where courts are involved it pays to step back and listen to the advice given by the professionals as opposed to a 'mate in the pub' who's been through it all. Think about all the implications

of separating from the mother of your children and follow a few
basic guidelines:

- Avoid making rash, heat-of-the-moment decisions or accusations.
- Try to keep things civil with your partner for the children's sake.
- Don't belittle or criticise your children's mother to them or in front
  of them – your feelings towards her may have changed, but ...
- ... remember that your kids are an innocent party and they need to
  remain children – avoid dragging them into the break-up wherever
  possible.
- Don't make the kids become go-betweens.

If you do move out or separate and your children are old enough
to understand, tell them that there is going to be a change in their
circumstances but reassure them that you and their mum will always
put them first and of course you'll always be their dad. You may stop
being husband and wife, but you will never stop being parents and so
should try to maintain a constructive ongoing relationship for their
sake. It is what is important for *them* that is most important of all.

Do whatever you can to reach an agreement without ending up
needing to go to court to seek a judge's view. Doing so only guarantees
that things will take longer and cost you more. If you find it hard
to talk to your wife without things getting heated then consider
mediation – it's not a soft option as some might think and it could
help you come to that agreement, or clarify the things you really need
legal advice on.

Milestone 86

Meeting your teenager's 'special one'
Age: 16 onwards

Use this cut-out-and-keep checklist to score your son or daughter's first 'brought-home-and-met-the-parents' boyfriend or girlfriend out of 10. Remember, for your child 'this is the ONE'. For them to have mustered up the courage to introduce their latest love to the family shows how much he or she means to them. Take it seriously, be welcoming and don't be too judgemental (note: use a pencil only to complete – just in case).

Marks out of 10

Characteristics	Girlfriend	Boyfriend
Punctuality when meeting		
Appearance when meeting		
Level of personal hygiene		
Level of sobriety		
Coherent use of language		
Clearly anxious		
Fearful		
Overly charming		
Flowers for mum/gift		

Characteristics	Girlfriend	Boyfriend
Eating habits		
Family background		
Career plans/prospects		
Son-/daughter-in-law potential		

DAD TALK: Rules for daughter's boyfriends

'I do have simple rules like keeping the bedroom door open whenever boyfriends visit and back home at sensible times – which they do test sometimes. So far the boyfriends have been polite, engaging and not like worst nightmare Kevin or Perry. I guess the thing I want is them to treat my girls like they are princesses and it does annoy me if they don't. You should try to meet the boyfriend at home and while being in control of the meeting, not intimidating them.'

Torre, father of Angel, Lily-Ann and Isabella

Milestone 87

Musical differences
Age: 13 onwards

You may find yourself asking 'Who stole my child?' on many occasions when a surly teen appears to have body-snatched the baby who once danced along happily to whatever you were tuned into. Teenage music choices can be a headache in more ways than one for parents – and they have been for generations. But in an age of streaming and earphones, YouTubers and influencers, the traditional scenario – kid tunes the car radio into something they like listening to, dad responds with a wry put-down – is becoming less and less common.

You're more likely to get an idea of what they're listening to at parties or gatherings at your home where they're in charge of the playlist – or just passing their bedroom door when they've got the speaker turned up to 11. What you hear may well shock you but before condemning them to a life of silence take a moment to consider what it would be like if you …

Don't switch off
Whether it's the noise, the genre or the lyrics you don't like the sound of, don't tune out completely. If you're concerned about what they're listening to, or just curious to work out exactly what the hell those lyrics are all about, get them to share it. It probably won't grow on you but if you take an interest they may respect your opinion a little more having at least given it a hearing.

Look at its merits
Your child's inexhaustible knowledge of an artist's lyrics, live shows, collaborations, personal habits and previous convictions should not only be admired for the passion they have for it, but should also even be actively encouraged if it's a potential career path into the multimillion-pound music industry or at least moonlighting as a DJ.

Dust off the CDs

Share some of the stuff you listened to when you were growing up by digging out your own collection or sourcing the soundtrack to your teenager years online. Sell this trip down memory lane to your youngster as a chance for them to discover music that influenced *their* favourite artists.

Do some chin-stroking

Use the opportunity of sharing your music with them to open up a discussion about 'the message in music' or 'what the artist is saying'. (Avoid sounding like a pretentious prat where possible.) Point out what your favourite songs were about and see if there's some common ground with the messages your kid's favourite artist is putting across.

You might not be able to change your kid's taste in music, or even really want to, but getting to listen to their music, understand what they like about it and even make them aware that you have a thought-through opinion on it – without totally annihilating the headline act that they adore – can mean you have a mutual topic for debate at a time when the act of communication between parents and teens is a rare occurrence.

189

Milestone 88

Political awakening
Age: 14

There's an old adage about never discussing politics, sex or religion in volatile settings where it could be inappropriate and lead to heated arguments or even violence – at the dinner table, in a pub, during the Women's Institute garden fair.

But as a role model, mentor and guide for your child throughout their life your wisdom in such matters may be called upon to help them deal with life's big questions. Church-going children will have doubts about faith at times. Be prepared for the 'If God exists then why ...' argument to come your way at times.

Also, as kids become more aware of their world, the part they play in it and the effect governments have upon their everyday life, they will start asking a fair few questions about the point of politicians, too (fair question). An NSPCC study in 2016 revealed a 35 per cent rise in children having counselling for anxiety – with issues such as Brexit, the Trump election and the Middle East cited by some kids as the topics most likely to keep them awake at night. You might not want to go through these matters at the dinner table – pick your moment – but don't follow that line about not discussing such matters at all. Instead engage them by ...

Playing politics at home
Quench your child's thirst for political discourse and the democratic process from an early age by putting the major decisions of the household to the vote. Teach them that the first-past-the-post system is how things work in the UK and that 'going to visit Nanna' has been chosen over 'going to Legoland' thanks to Mum having the casting vote.

Teach them the significance

Seriously, press home the importance of voting from an early age. Taking them along to political marches, letting them stand for class rep and chatting about political items on the news and what it may mean for them and their friends – without terrifying them – will help politics feel more relevant to them. And it may even help you to make some sense of it all, too.

Let them be the leader

Don't soapbox your 16-year-old about 'why a vote for the Greens is a wasted one' or how 'it doesn't matter who – they're all the same'. It's always a better idea to let children lead the debate. Let them ask the questions and you answer succinctly – avoiding your own bias coming through if you can – then wait for them to glaze over or start looking at their phone.

Maybe check with them later or the next day to see if they have any more questions or thoughts on monetary policy, town planning or war with China, just to keep the topic live.

Milestone 89

In the eyes of the law
Age: 16th birthday

Your child's 16th birthday is a landmark occasion which comes with a whole host of new legal status 'gifts'. They're unlikely to get overly excited about most of them – but you should both be aware of these rights all the same. Depending on where in the world you live these will vary, but among the changes your child can enjoy when they turn 16 in the UK are:

Good laws

Marriage – at 16 your son or daughter can get married, including same-sex marriage. They're at the age of consent for sex, but it's illegal for a person in a position of trust or power (e.g. a teacher) to have sex with someone under the age of 18.

Education and welfare – at 16 they're eligible for free full-time education (at school or sixth-form college). They'll also get their National Insurance number through the post with their birthday cards, which means they can claim benefits if needs be.

World of work – at 16 they can earn the minimum wage, invest in a cash ISA and join the Army, though they'll still need your consent to do this last one. Try not to appear too keen when they ask to join-up by offering to pack their Bergen and polish their boots for them.

Bad laws

Leave home – at 16 they're legally able to leave home, and you're legally able to ask them to do so. Social Services may intervene if you do, or apply for a care order to see that they're looked after at least until they're 17.

Medical treatment – as of their 16th birthday they no longer need you to give consent to medical, dental and surgical treatment. They can choose their own doctor too – which is no bad thing, but it does mean they can now sell their kidney to buy an iPad – as at least one teenager has done.

Ride a 50cc moped (with a provisional licence) – freedom, independence, learning essential road skills ... just some of the things your neighbours won't be thinking of when YOUR kid starts tearing around the estate riding what sounds like a souped-up lawnmower.

Just mad laws...

They're not old enough to vote as yet, despite now being legally able to lay down their life for Queen, country and government as a soldier. But your 16-year-old child can now drink beer, cider or a glass of wine with a meal in a restaurant, gamble (buy a National Lottery ticket) and fly a glider ... Preferably not all at once.

Milestone 90

Teaching your teen to drive
Age: 17 onwards

In a bid to reduce the amount spent on driving lessons or just to put an end to their pestering, you may find yourself at some point letting your teen drive your car. It might be a spin around an empty car park – just so they get a feel for the basics – but once their instructor feels they're ready to go out on the road then the pressure will be on for you to give them lessons, too – cursing the aforementioned instructor while you do.

Dave Dunsford, driving instructor at RED Driving School and a dad, has plenty of experience of introducing kids to the wheel of his car – including his own. He suggests you do the following before allowing your offspring to give it a try:

- 'Wait until the instructor says your teen is ready to go out with you. Chat with their instructor who will (unbeknownst to you) be sounding out whether YOU are safe enough for your kid to drive with.'

- 'It's a good idea to practise on roads you both know well – so probably ones the instructor uses, but before you go decide on what area to cover – MSM or parking, say – as opposed to just driving down to the shops.'

- 'Know your limitations too. If you child hasn't done dual carriageway driving with their instructor yet, it's not really the time to give it a go. Remember your instructor's car will have dual controls, yours won't.'

- 'When I was teaching my daughter to drive I did what I advise other parents to do. Imagine that you have someone else, a friend of theirs, in the rear seat too. That should help keep things good-natured.'

- 'Check your insurance – ensuring that you're OK to take them out in your car. There are age restrictions as to who can teach someone else to drive, too.'
- 'Rehearse your instructions when you're driving alone, too. How much time do you give yourself to turn at the next junction? Say it aloud when approaching and then imagine how much time a novice driver will need.'
- 'Encourage them all the time by focusing on what they're doing well – it's a learning process, so they will make mistakes; your role is to help them build on their strengths, boost their confidence on the road and get more familiar with driving. The instructor will iron out those errors.'

Milestone 91

Funding student lifestyles

Age: 16 onwards

Before your child is finally able to pay their way through life they're going to need a helping hand-out or two along the way. In the UK, until the age of 16, many families receive Child Benefit to contribute to the cost of raising each child. However, if your child goes on to further education they won't receive any state support as such.

You'll see some of the costs of their student lifestyle coming. More than 50 per cent of young people in the UK now go on to university and while they are offered loans to pay for some of the cost of living and studying – which are paid back when they're working and earning above a certain amount – it's worth knowing in advance that there's a 'parental contribution' cost too. Based upon what you earn – your family income – you may be expected to top up their student living loan with some funds of your own.

Dad tales: Topping up their loan

‘ Money is also something to consider, we gave our eldest an amount each a month for "food" when she went off to Uni – not a massive amount but more than many can afford. Thankfully she had savings from working over the holidays – don't expect the loan alone to cover everything. ’

Torre, father of Angel, Lily-Ann and Isabella

The TV financial guru Martin Lewis of www.MoneySavingExpert. com suggests that as a rule of thumb the maximum amount you would need to contribute at the moment based on the parental contribution – you can always give them more – is around £5000 ($6150) a year (or nearly £6000/($7370 if your child is going to uni in London). On a three-year course that would be £15,000 ($18,500). 'The key factor is family income. Roughly, if it's over around £60,000 ($73,700) then start preparing to save £15,000 ($18,500). If your total family income is under £25,000 ($30,700), you don't need to save anything. If your family income is in the middle, £45,000 ($55,280), you want to be saving around £7800 ($9580) for your kids to go to university.'

The student loan system is liable to change but at the time of writing a few factors for parents to consider include:

- Tuition fees – up to £9,250 ($11,360) a year – are paid for by the Student Loans Company.
- Over a typical three-year course the combined loan for fees and living costs can be up to £50k ($61.5k).
- Your son or daughter will only repay the student loan once they've left uni and earn £25,725+ ($31,600+) (and with the current terms that threshold is set to rise each year in line with average earnings). They'll then repay 9 per cent of earnings over that £25,725 ($31,600) figure. (The loan is wiped after 30 years – whether you've paid a penny or not.)

Ways to save

Lewis suggests students also look at ways of easing the cost of their studies by investigating student-specific bank accounts, education grants, council tax and retail store discounts (via websites like StudentBeans), along with rail and travel reductions and switching utility and mobile phone suppliers.

Milestone 92

Further education: a father's role
Age: 17 onwards

You may think your primary role at this stage of your kid's life is predominantly one of supporting them via your dwindling bank balance, but the cost of college or university life isn't the only demand dads and mums face when a child goes on to further education, especially when it takes them away from the family home. The opportunities for them taking the next step towards independence are wonderful of course, plus it's – in theory – a step towards a career, plus you're no longer being woken at 3 a.m. by a drunk teenager who's lost their key or is noisily plundering the fridge. But it's another milestone moment that can shake the family foundations.

University crash course

Once they've been accepted and are sorting out their digs, help out with a crash course in the stuff they usually ask you to do: basic cooking, how to separate laundry colours (read a washing label), essential food hygiene and 'use by' dates, wiring plugs, etc. Also, so that they don't blow their entire loan, bursary or nest egg you've saved for them during freshers' week, a lesson in budgeting and money management could well be worthwhile.

Don't pop the corks just yet

Avoid advertising their bedroom on Airbnb for a moment, too. The first few weeks of student life away from home can take some getting used to. Your son or daughter may be back for home visits sooner than you expected – don't encourage it but obviously let them know that they're always welcome ... no matter how much you enjoy the peace.

Bed and board

Cost is one of the key factors behind more and more sons and daughters deciding to study at a university near home. Not moving out at all – but not being in full-time work or even eligible for Child Benefit – can throw up new problems. Can they contribute to the family budget or at least play a role in keeping the family home tidy when they're still living there? If they're not moving out, are there opportunities for local part-time work – to support their lifestyle and contribute towards their bed and board?

All change

The trauma of having a child move away can hit parents hard, but also consider how it affects any siblings. They may not be as prepared for it as you and they'll struggle to cope even more if you're making out that it's the end of the world.

Having a child head off to university can leave parents feeling like there's a big kid-sized gap in their lives for the first time in 17 years or so. It's not uncommon for parental splits to occur at this time – university counselling services even acknowledge this by calling the post-Christmas rise in requests for help from students coming to terms with their parents separating a 'January timebomb'. Those same counsellors suggests that by discovering new activities, hobbies or ventures the pair of you can do together you can help prevent that sense of 'loss' or the reassessment of your relationship taking a more destructive path.

Milestone 93

Their gap year of discovery

Age: 18 onwards

Your child going off to 'find themselves', take a gap year or discover parts of the world where wi-fi isn't on tap should generally be encouraged – or at least grudgingly supported – as your son or daughter takes the next step towards growing into a worldly wise and rounded young person. It's a great chance to broaden their horizons, learn self-sufficiency, meet new people, even try out jobs and experience other cultures. 'Backpacking' always looks good on a CV and a child who heads off even for just a few months will return more resilient and woke.

Knowing all this, of course, doesn't stop parents wondering and worrying, which is why some of the best advice if your child is heading off overseas with a passport, pants and half-baked plan includes ...

Contact calls

Agree on the best method for your young adventurer to keep in touch with you and how regularly they will do this. Arranging to call home at set times each week or so may not work but having some form of contact – phone or Skype calls, social media messages and even letters or postcards – will help ease your worries and give them some comfort, too.

Do their homework

Get involved in their planning and help them research their route – they may have fixed plans about where they want to go and who with, but they will probably still need some pointers on money, security and country customs they're not aware of. Questions about how long they plan to go for, what their 'goals' might be and what to do if they get into any bother should be part of the planning chat, too. They also need to make sure they get visas and vaccinations sorted in good time, and be aware that these cost money and have to be done at a certain time before they can enter a country.

Hook them up

The established networks for backpackers will help them find places to stay and even work en route, but if you have friends or relatives you can put them in touch with in different parts of the world then build that into the plan. Check that you've got up-to-date contact details for them.

Meet their mates

If they're travelling with companions make a point of meeting them too – even if it's just for a 'farewell party'. Having their contact details or being in touch with their parents can be a further reassurance.

Work their passage

Encourage them to self-fund their trip as much as possible. They'll value the money they have more if they've put some toil into getting it.

Prepare to be flexible

Both parents and kids should know that no matter how well planned out their travel plans are, it's never quite going to go the way they anticipate. There may be some hiccups along the way – which makes the experience invaluable but a little worrisome at times. Preparing them as best you can, and making sure they can get in contact if there are any problems, can put a few minds at rest. Let them know that there's no shame in coming home early or postponing their trip if needs be, too.

Milestone 94

Sending your kid off to work
Age: 16 onwards

When your son or daughter completes school, college or university the next step into the world of work may well require some fatherly guidance. The chances are that they've been in some form of employment during their studies – part-time or a work placement linked to their course. Their university careers service will offer some practical tips, but breaking into the world of full-time work is a whole new venture that requires application (lots of applications) plus resilience to deal with the knock-backs. Their self-esteem may take a bit of a pounding if they don't land a job straight away and this, coupled with them possibly having to move back home after a few years of living independently, could cause things to become a little tense. Some support from the home front may be needed more than ever. Here are a few pointers to help you deal with the situation:

- Do reassure them. They'll feel the pressure to get on the career ladder, so give them some words of encouragement – draw on your own experiences if they're relevant.
- Don't nag them, or make them feel like they're a burden (even if they are). Some persuasion is good, and don't let any bad habits take root while they're looking for work, but they will want to work, earn and regain their full independence ASAP so focus on that rather than the dirty laundry and trail of toast crumbs.
- Do push the positive. The dream job doesn't come without a few nightmares along the way, so let them know that they may have to take a job they're not overly keen on just to get them into the world of networking and gainful employment.

- Don't take over. You can't necessarily find the right job for them, and you shouldn't. They're going to be doing the job, not you. Offer to read through applications but don't write them or contact companies on your kid's behalf.
- Do use contacts. You might be able to put them in touch with friends or associates in the line of work they want to get into. It may be for work experience, an internship or just some insider advice – all of which may help get their foot in the door. Make the offer to help or pass on the number but let your child take it from there.

Be positive

Being out of work can have a serious impact on your child's mental health. Anxiety around money, sense of worth and status can gnaw away at their confidence. They may even feel like spending years at uni or college wasn't the right move. Let them know that employers will always value a degree or diplomas and the sacrifice made towards getting them, and that the life experience itself will have been useful, as they'll discover in time.

Milestone 95

Child takes over the family business

Age: 21 onwards

It's the stuff that business empires are made of. Your offspring have learned all they know about the cut and thrust from the old master himself and now you're ready to bequeath the home laundry dynasty to him or her knowing that the next generation will make it a global operation. But before you sit back and watch the kids pick it up and run with it, contemplate how you groomed them to be your business successor in the first place. Going into business with your children with a view to passing your empire on to them can change the shape of the father–child relationship – not least when they realise you've been bluffing your way through work as well as fatherhood for all these years. Nevertheless, there are some sound reasons why you should consider adding '& Son' or 'Johnson & Johnson' to the family firm …

It's an upgrade of you
New ideas, more energy, different skills – there are plenty of strengths your son or daughter could bring to your business. If they're a chip off the old block then they'll hopefully have some of the vigour and drive you had when you started out – plus a whole load more technology know-how or modern marketing skills.

You'll keep it close
It could be that your already strong relationship makes them an ideal business partner. You're both going to be putting in some long hours with all the ups and downs that come with earning a livelihood – who better to have watching your back than one of your own? Alternatively, it could be the business that bonds you – giving you a shared interest and a respect for each other that goes beyond the family obligations.

Just 42 per cent of UK family businesses have any form of succession planning in place – with only 30 per cent surviving the transition to the second generation and 10 per cent to the third, according to a survey by Legal & General in 2018. It might not seem like a priority when you're playing in the park with your kid but there's a school of thought that says it's never too early to introduce them to the family business ...

Big up the job

Avoid bitching about work around them. They easily detect tensions in the family, especially ones linked to finance or 'another tough day at the office'. Don't put them off the thought of working with you before you've even thought of it yourself.

Don't make it a given

It may have been in the family for generations but don't assume it'll be your kid who takes it over. When talking to them about career paths, make it clear to them that they really do have a choice. Insisting it's not a guaranteed shoo-in to the family firm also encourages them to strive and prove themselves.

Let them learn on someone else's time

It could benefit you in the long run to let them go out and work for another company before you put them on the payroll at your firm. They'll pick up ideas and gain credibility that they may need when it comes to dealing with other employees at 'Daddy's firm'.

Give it some thought

Of course it's got its pitfalls too. You're emotionally invested in the business for starters – plus the friction that occurs in every workplace can make home life hellish. Discussing budget forecasts for the next quarter will put the mockers on the Christmas dinner, too. Think long and hard before agreeing to develop a dynasty.

Milestone 96

Fond farewell
Age: 23

Twenty-three is the first age at which more than 50 per cent of young people had left the parental home, according to a survey in 2017. That's not to say they won't be back again at some point, but once they've got the means to make money for themselves and possibly want a space of their own – to share with someone else – be prepared for the next, more 'hands-off' phase of fatherhood to begin.

If you thought your kid's first day at school was a significant step in the direction of independence then the day they leave home to move into a place of their own will feel like an earth-shattering life change for you. This kind of goodbye may well have been something you've experienced before if they've already moved away to go to uni or else have been spending more and more time staying with a partner and decided that it's time to take the plunge. It can be exciting and a little unnerving for them, and for parents it can trigger a sense of loss or a lack of purpose. What's more, because we're usually popping champagne corks at the time of their departure the true gravity of what's happening may not hit home right away. It comes with the day-to-day reality afterwards that they are no longer living with you – especially when there are no siblings there either – and can be the hardest part.

Move them on
If they're moving away some distance then giving them some practical help can be comforting. They may welcome you driving them and their stuff to their new home or going with them on public transport. The offer of helping out with any decorating or moving them into a new home may help ease the transition, too.

Plan a party

Not quite a celebration, more an opportunity for friends and relatives
to help send them on their way. Talk to them first before holding
anything like a leaving party – but certainly sow the seed in the mind
of those who are heading off overseas.

Contract for contact

If you're helping to move them in, agree beforehand how long you are
going to stay for. Make arrangements about who will call who each
week, and when. Striking a balance between being on hand to help
out while not being too clingy may take some working out. They'll be
reassured to know you're there for them but won't want you dropping
by for a cuppa every day.

The physical separation from your child and the act of them moving
out can be quite an upheaval, but for many parents that's not the
hardest part. No longer having that daily involvement in their lives
can make some parents anxious. Staying in touch and keeping the
communication flowing without being overwhelming will help combat
those inevitable feelings of loneliness and loss.

Milestone 97

Dealing with the empty nest

Age: 19 onwards

Rolwand, father of Tom and Sam

'As the boys got older, took exams and started thinking about careers, I became very mindful that I needed to experience as much as I could with them because they would be leaving home. When the time came there was the anticipation of the empty house, how I would cope without them and a realisation that I needed to rebuild my relationship with my wife as she was going through similar thoughts and experiences.

'I was preoccupied with the logistics of moving them, finding a place, and finally the journey down to university. I remember being quiet in the car, not knowing what to say, and everything I did say was stupid or irrelevant and annoying to them. I tried too hard to make it a "normal" transition to them leaving home. It was a very emotional, sad and upsetting yet proud experience. My boys are making it along the path of development. Home was empty. It felt cold and quiet and I hated it.

'We didn't say much to each other, either on the journey back or when we were home. I went upstairs and saw their rooms empty. Is it best to close their bedroom doors or keep them open so it can seem like they might just be out? It was such an eerie atmosphere, something that you cannot prepare for, and took some getting used to.

'We redecorated and tried to give a fresh uplift to the house to try to alleviate the "loss" and make it nice for when they came home. My dad just dropped me off at digs in Leicester and said "bye" and that was all the contact we had other than a quick 10p phone call. That must have been tough, but we never spoke about it and the experience he went through. Now, social media has bridged that gap and we're in almost constant contact. I suppose it brought us together more, but in a perverse way it made it difficult because it meant I missed them more.

'But the hard part was almost the re-inventing of the relationship with my wife and the adjustments needed to support all the anxieties over our sons. The need to talk about ourselves and the boys – with the latter taking the dominant role. It is important to take a step back and work through this phase together. There was a temptation to feel sorry for myself because of how close I am to them, but really I was positive in my outlook to the situation and had support around from friends who were going through the same thing. I recognised the need to be strong and share the experience for the good of myself and my family.'

Milestone 98

Rediscovering life after the kids have left

Age: 23 onwards

Media reporting of the experiences of parents who dearly miss their kids when they leave home for university, jobs or marriage often highlights the negatives. The empty nest syndrome is often portrayed as a time when long-married couples suddenly discover the only thing they had in common was the kids. But for many it's a time to kick back and enjoy a whole new, hands-off form of parenting. You have greater freedom to enjoy and fewer responsibilities. Often, in fact, the marriage gets better – not because couples were miserable when the kids were around, just that they've suddenly got a fresh impetus. Only when the kids have gone do some dads and mums realise that they should have carved out more stress-free time with each other years ago. Empty nesters can fill their time again in a variety of ways ...

Take time out

In the maelstrom of your kid moving out and all the fraught emotions that go with it the pair of you may have suffered a touch of emotional burn-out. Taking a break or even using the new-found freedom to head off on that dream holiday is one way of rewarding yourselves for a couple of decades of devoted parenting and provides a chance to rekindle your pre-child passions.

Let the dust settle

As tempting as it may be to downsize and sell up and take yourself off on the nomadic lifestyle you've only fantasised about before, it's a good idea to delay any drastic changes. Everyone needs a bit of time to adjust to the new situation – particularly your child, who may have to return at some point.

Get out of the house

While it might not be a good idea to relocate the family home right away it's definitely an ideal time to fill any free time with some new activities. Discovering new interests or sports together that get the endorphins flowing and open up a new social circle can make dealing with your children moving out a little easier, too.

Dad tales: What to do when they've gone...

' Having helped both lads through the education system in one way or another we had some very large loans to pay off. It only struck me as we drove Peter up to his new digs that we were now on our own, and that a big chapter of my life had closed, I had no children any more; I had two grown-up lads who were not at home anymore. The best way I could resolve this was simply to keep looking forwards, not back, and plan the future for my wife and I. But we were also broke. The answer was to let out two bedrooms to foreign students coming to the UK – over the years it has slowly helped us pull back the debts. It is very odd at first having other people in your house – but you become a sort of surrogate father and mother. It would not suit many couples as the house dynamics and your own relationship changes. **'**

Paul, father of Sam and Peter

Milestone 99

Boomerang kid comes back
Age: 23 onwards

In 2017, nearly a million more young adults in the UK were living with their parents than were in 1997 (according to a survey by Civitas). Right now, it's estimated that on average one in four 20–34-year-olds now live at home. In London, thanks to the cost of private rents and housing, that figure rises to 41 per cent. These young adults who've had to return home – after living independently as students or when starting work or relationships – have been called the 'boomerang generation'.

It's an arrangement that can have its ups and downs and one that, in an ideal world, neither you nor your son or daughter really want. Issues around privacy, house rules and social life can flare up – possibly again if you went through all this in the teenage years. Living with your 30-something-year-old child won't be so different at times but it pays to agree a few ground rules first. Sit down, open up a bottle and have a mature, amiable discussion.

They're not alone

Terms like 'boomerangers' don't help the situation. Labelling the many young men and women as such can add to the feeling of shame that they have to live back home with Mum and Dad again. It's perceived by some as being some sort of failure to make it in the world. In reality, the economics of living alone, especially during a housing shortage, means your child is doing what millions of others their age have to do around the world.

Agree a fee

If your child is saving for a deposit for a place of their own you may feel reluctant to accept money from them towards their board and keep. If you can afford to help them out in that way, it'll shorten their stay, but by moving back with you and your partner they're increasing the population of the house considerably. When it's put that way, it should be a given that they contribute something to the cost of their food, heating, phone bills, etc., if they're earning a living.

Allow some space

Aside from having their old bedroom back – and hopefully keeping it a lot tidier than before – look at ways of making your home life more comfortable when there are more adults in it. Creating more living space – extensions, garage annexes or loft conversions – is one option, or just give each other some time alone at home each week by setting up schedules when either parents or child head out for an evening.

Set a time frame

Don't be surprised if you don't find yourself jumping through hoops at the thought of you child moving back in with you. You've adjusted to your new life – with the freedoms, space and full fridge once again – then suddenly it's put on hold as you've got the pitter-patter of adult feet following you around the house. Researchers even found that mothers' and fathers' quality of life decreased when one of their offspring moved back – according to a US study from the journal *Social Science and Medicine*. Setting a target for when they may be able to move out again can give everyone a light at the end of a sometimes overcrowded tunnel.

Milestone 100

Establishing boundaries with your adult kids

Age 18 and over

Maintaining a great relationship with your offspring as they reach adulthood – regardless of whether they're living with you or not – may call for some compromise. Cross that line between caring and overbearing and you're in for trouble.

Parents who want to be 'best friends' with their grown-up son or daughter can be in for a nasty surprise when, even though their kid is much more mature (in theory at least), they still kick-off randomly or justifiably don't want mum or dad involved in certain aspects of their lives. Setting the boundaries of this friendship takes time but it's essential to enjoy fulfilling, fun and occasionally friction-filled moments together for years to come.

Draw lines of communication – Some parents have telephone chats with their adult kids every day. Some will text each other throughout the week. Others won't speak for months on end. Establish a contact routine that works for you all – a routine catch-up call for both parties to share news and gossip, pass on dates or events to remember and generally keep the communication lines open. Agree visits in advance, avoid turning up unannounced and remember though, this has to work both ways – accommodate to your kid's needs but don't let them dictate your life either.

Beware the bombshell boundary breakers – Passing judgement on your kid's lifestyle habits, relationship decisions, career choices or financial frivolity is guaranteed to cause rows and even alienation. Give advice when it's called for, or if you're really concerned about something that requires one of those 'difficult conversations' take a leaf out of the management manuals; firstly, pick your moment to raise an issue. Prepare the points you want to make then ask your son or daughter if they can make a time to discuss the matter. Be open-minded. Air your concerns and emphasise that you've got their best interests at heart. Listen. No, really listen. Don't end without a clean conclusion – even if you agree to disagree do at least agree. Avoidance isn't a great way of dealing with conflict within families, things just fester.

Manage your media – Social media can be a major source of angst between friends, work colleagues and definitely families. If you're a social sharing type online do talk with your kids about their feelings on being featured in posts – especially pics of any grandchildren. Speaking of grandchildren, a couple of no-no's to avoid when the time comes include...

- Offer advice only when asked. Grown-up sons and daughters may turn to their parents for advice and support when they have children of their own. But just as you probably learnt much about parenthood through trial and error, so your kids should too. Be wary of enforcing your parenting ethos on them or criticising the way they raise your grandchildren – it's a guaranteed way to cause resentment and jeopardise the relationships you have with everyone.
- Be sure to ask about your kid first. When you contact your adult offspring be sure to inquire about them first before asking how the grandchildren are. As obvious as that sounds it's a trap many fall into.

Milestone 101

Dad's midlife crisis
Age: 18 onwards

The male midlife crisis, or 'dadolescence' as it's been called, can occur at any stage along the fatherhood journey, though the 'mid-life' tag acknowledges that it's usually when your kids are moving on and you've suddenly got more time to reflect on where you're at. It's loosely defined as being when dad 'loses it a bit'.

First identified in the mid-1960s and investigated by psychologist Carl Jung, this 'crisis' reportedly manifests itself in a variety of forms. These range from taking up new hobbies and activities, getting nostalgic for past passions, feeling like you're in a rut, and conducting a makeover of one's looks and clothing, to shelling out on that 'dream' purchase (Harley-Davidson motorbikes are a popular one), quitting your job and taking up the career you always wanted, or embarking on an illicit affair with a younger woman. Or all of these and worse.

However, the peddlers of these stereotypes fail to realise that this is just another rite of passage on the fatherhood journey and far from being a crisis, it is really a state of transition – the 'dadolescence' term suits this state as it's like a second teenage period. Fathers going through it should seize it and treat it as a celebration of all they've achieved so far as role models, mentors and men of action when it came to raising their kids. When you hit this point be sure to do the following:

Go outside your comfort zone
Trying out new activities, taking up new sports, increasing your knowledge, learning a new language or going travelling all capitalise on that restless spirit the 'crisis' creates. Putting it to some constructive use – especially when it's a healthy habit that can combat some of the physical changes men are prone to after they're 35, such as a dip in testosterone – can reap plenty of rewards.

Set some new targets

Find something that can bring some new energy into your career or a spark into your marriage, channelling the time you used to devote to the kids to engage in relationship-enhancing hobbies. Work up a list of things together that you want to accomplish in the next year or two or five – from home projects to new personal goals, and discuss how they can be achieved.

'Have more kids'

They kept you young, active and time-fulfilled, why not get some more? That doesn't mean having more of your own or even adopting, but volunteering with groups that help kids learn about life – Scouts, explorers, and youth and sports associations cry out for positive male role models. You may have skills that can assist schools or provide foster care.

See the positives

While the word 'crisis' can suggest it's all doom and gloom at this time of life, it's actually a fresh opportunity to look at what you want from life and how your role as a parent will be changing. As a couple, you may find this time much more challenging, but whatever path you take, you're a father for life and you'll still have a huge influence on your children's lives, albeit from a distance now.

Milestone 102

Giving them away ...
Age: 18 and over

Of course you'll always be their 'daddy', 'pa', 'the old man' or whatever title your kids bestow upon you, but there may come a point when you – as father of the bride or groom – give them an official send-off to a new life with their chosen partner. Your child may not go for something as formal as a marriage – where you walk them down an aisle or at least accompany them on their stag night – but if they do, and you're called upon to give your blessing, stump up a dowry, shell out for the ceremony or simply get up at the reception and wish them all the best, you may want a few pointers to help you, and them, on the way ...

Father of the bride or groom
Saying your bit during the post-nuptial speeches is a traditional role and increasingly one that the father of the groom gets asked to play a part in too these days. You don't have to be the world's greatest stand-up comic – the best man is there for that. Instead, you give thanks and celebrate the joy your child has brought to your life ... before palming them off on someone else. Work out your own words; the speech doesn't have to be long but it does help if it comes from the heart. All the best dad's speeches include:

- A solid intro. Welcome the guests, compliment the supporting cast and crack a joke if you want to help settle a few nerves.
- Pull out a story. A sweet, amusing or downright hilarious anecdote about your son or daughter is customary – childhood nicknames, school incidents, memorable moments, etc. – but remember that it's their big day so avoid going over the top with embarrassing tales and keep any mention of ex-partners to a minimum, if at all.

- Sing their praises. Whether you end up taking the piss out of them or not, try to work the speech back round to highlighting the qualities you adore about them and how fortunate your new son- or daughter-in-law is to have them – don't forget to say a kind word or two about the son- or daughter-in-law also.
- Sign off with wisdom. Finally, impart some fatherly, worldly advice – drawn from your long experience – before raising a toast to 'the happy couple!'

Milestone 103

From good father, to Godfather

Fair enough, you don't have to be a father to be chosen as a godfather. But as an established dad your fatherly status, your air of maturity and your proven ability to at least tolerate kids (your own and other people's) for any length of time means you're more likely to get chosen to have this honour over other feckless wonders in your coterie of mates.

Traditionally – dating back to the 9th century AD – it's been the role of the godfather to oversee a child's spiritual instruction. Sure enough, if the child's parents so wish, you can carry out that part of the job description to the best of your abilities. (The parents' chosen church will have a bluffer's guide of some sort for you). But for most godfathers the role is much more secular these days. It's nothing like the Mafia-heavy version in the film of the same name – although your commitment to the job over time will determine if you're a lowly foot-soldier, a mid-range capo or a highly respected top boss in the Godfather stakes. Here's what you need to do to reach such heights:

Step 1: Attend the christening/ceremony. A sure-fire way of getting this Godfather-Godchild relationship off to a flying start is be there when called upon. Attending the christening plus any rehearsal and getting familiar with your role on the day by doing some homework will all win you brownie points. If the parents are hosting a less formal, 'welcoming ceremony' it's your chance to shine as godfather by looking smart in the photos, remembering the kid's name, making a short speech on how you'll be there to support your godchild for years to come and bringing a gift.

Step 2: Remember their milestone moments. Making a note in the diary each year to send your godchild a birthday gift and ensuring they're on the festive gift list each year marks you out as a godfather with dedication. Adult friends can lose touch over time but by fulfilling your role to this extent you'll not only be cherished by the godchild but also always in the thoughts of the parents who lumbered you with the job in the first place.

Step 3: Act as a mentor. In an age of increasingly mobile, transient nuclear families going wherever the work is it can be hard for parents to call upon reliable adult support. It's also tough for kids growing up with only their parents and teachers as acceptable adult role models. Step forward *THE* godfather. Mentoring your godchild, taking an active interest in their academic or sporting success, taking them out for days with your own family, nurturing their talents, fostering a trusting relationship and basically being a handy bloke to have around for the kid and their parents shows a true mastery of this role.

Step 4: Raise them as your own. Tradition again. In the past godparents were given first refusal on a godchild whose parents had died unexpectedly – plague etc, etc. Nowadays this commitment would put you in the Godfather Elite, but before you start having any second thoughts you should know that there really *isn't* a legal obligation in the UK for godparents to do this anymore.

Milestone 104

Dad becomes Grandad...

You've only just got used to being called dad and suddenly you're told there's someone on the way who's going to be calling you 'Grandpa' or 'Grampy' or 'Pops' forever more. Aside from the misplaced idea that this suddenly makes you ancient – the average age for a first-time grandparent in the UK is just 49 – becoming a grandparent often marks a whole new chapter in the lives of parents – introducing them or taking them back to experiences they've not enjoyed for years. The key things to know, which will help you readily adjust to your new-found role is that it's a whole new ball game – literally when they start toddling and you're looking after them. It's a great opportunity for families to build better relationships – or repair fractured ones – as the grandchildren act like a bonding substance. (Similar to the glue you'll now keep in your 'Pop's' shed along with other assorted tools.) To enjoy it further, here's some grandfatherly advice for you:

Grandad Tales

‘ Although there's quite a geographical distance between my son's place and my home (Manchester and London) I do get to see Eric a lot because I travel to London every week with work. I was absolutely over the moon to discover I was going to be a grandfather and I'm as involved as I can be. Being a younger grandad is great too – hopefully I'll be around for a long time to see Eric grow up and get to know him. My son sends me pictures all the time so I get to see my grandson's constant development plus I get to Skype my son and see Eric too – he's a really happy little boy – and these days it's easier to be involved and stay in touch. It's not only been a major enhancement to the great relationship I have with my son but it's also brought me closer to his wife too – it's given us all a chance to bond on another level. ’

Martin, 56, grandfather to Eric

❝ The twins were born premature and kept in ICU for weeks – it was heart-breaking not being able to cuddle them. When they came home we took turns to stay at my daughter's house to assist her with feeding, etc. We help her out as much as we can and we have the twins stay with us over a few weekends to give our daughter some rest and allow her to catch up on sleep. I love it that they both recognise my voice as soon as I walk in the room, they look around for me and I am greeted with the most amazing smiles, which is so heart-warming. It's very important to listen to how their mother wants them to be treated and raised; for example sticking to routines at bed time and naps throughout the day, it may not be my way but they are my grandchildren not my children (there is a difference). We can advise when asked for our opinion or input but we must not expect our way to be adhered too, and it's up to my daughter to make her own decisions. ❞

Steve, 49, grandfather to twins Nellie-Rae and Freddie

❝ We love taking Willow out in her pram and I love the idea of becoming a mentor as she grows up, not trying to be a parent but taking a step back and providing her with perspective and being a wise counsel. I think my generation is a lot younger and fitter than my grandparents' generation. Since Willow was born, I have become more concerned about the environment and what we leave behind for her generation. Also Willow is mixed race and it has made me think more deeply about intolerance and I hate the thought of her ever being abused because of her skin colour. The advice I would give to other grandparents is don't try and be a parent, take a step back and let her mum and dad learn the ropes as we did. Be on hand to offer support and guidance. ❞

Pau, 55, grandfather to Willow

Father ahead

Fatherhood has changed beyond all recognition when compared with the role a few generations ago. Today, as dads we're increasingly and rightly encouraged to be actively involved in every element of raising our children. Workplaces, policies and attitudes are shifting to enable this to happen more and more. Whether its flexible working and parental leave, dad's clubs or even baby changing facilities that aren't just located in the women's toilet, the importance of a dad's place in raising a child is finally being acknowledged.

It's important that the changes continue because, as I hope you've seen from this book and your own experiences, dads really are different. The way we play with our kids, the influences we have, the bonds we form – all differ greatly from the way mums do things.

Never underestimate your influence upon your child and your role as a father – throughout your child's life. The bonds you build and the habits that form in the early stages of fatherhood will set the template for the relationship you have with your children for years to come. Not only that, but it will have a crucial influence upon how they interact with their own offspring too one day.

My experiences of new fatherhood involved plenty of mishaps and learning on the job. Yours will too. The need to be a good dad has never been greater, either. Today's world is crying out for positive male role models to guide and nurture children from birth and well into adulthood – protecting them and preparing them, giving them tools to deal with all that life throws their way.

As I said at the beginning, not all the examples you've read here will be ones you'll experience – there will be many more moments of joy and sorrow along the way that are unique to you. But I hope that by having read *Dadding It!* you're a little more prepared for the lifelong journey that is fatherhood. Above all else, give it your best shot and be there for them in whatever way you can. Good luck.

Acknowledgements

A huge thank you to everyone credited throughout the book for their advice and input. Many thanks also to the fathers, of all ages, who contributed their tips, wisdom and experience. Thanks to Daddilife, Dadsnet and the Fatherhood Institute – along with the many dad bloggers and authors for the important work that you do.

Finally, a big thank you to Matthew Lowing, Sarah Skipper and all at Bloomsbury Publishing for their guidance and patience.

Useful resources for dads

Health

Addaction UK
Provides guidance on substance abuse for parents
www.addaction.org.uk/

Red Cross course
First aid for babies and children
www.redcrossfirstaidtraining.co.uk/Courses/First-aid-public-courses/First-aid-for-baby-and-child.aspx

St John Ambulance courses
www.sja.org

NHS UK
Children's health and medical conditions
www.nhs.uk/conditions/social-care-and-support-guide/caring-for-children-and-young-people/children-and-young-peoples-services/

Support

National Childbirth Trust
Support charity for parents
www.nct.org.uk/

Family Lives Helpline
Parenting and family support
0808 800 2222
www.familylives.org.uk/advice/teenagers/behaviour/

Bullying UK
Part of the Family Lives support service
www.bullying.co.uk/

Relate
Parenting teenagers advice
www.relate.org.uk/relationship-help/help-family-life-and-parenting/parenting-teenagers

Young Minds
Counselling Services For Children and Young People
https://youngminds.org.uk/find-help/for-parents/parents-guide-to-support-a-z/parents-guide-to-support-counselling-services/

MIND
Where adults, children and young people can get help and support for mental health issues
www.mind.org.uk/information-support/for-children-and-young-people/XRCNXetKiUk

NSPCC
In addition to their other work, the NSPCC provides guidance about internet safety and bullying
www.nspcc.org.uk

Childcare
Sitters
Online babysitting service
www.sitters.co.uk

Bloom Childcare + Coworking
Coworking network designed specifically for families
www.bloomchildcareandcoworking.com/

Babysitting Apps
Yoopies
Bambino
UrbanSitter

Education
Oxford Owl
Advice and educational resources for primary-age children
www.oxfordowl.co.uk

The school run
Educational resources and information for primary-age children
www.theschoolrun.com

Explore Learning
Tuition and courses
www.explorelearning.co.uk/blog

BBC Bitesize
Help with revision, exams and learning
www.bbc.co.uk/bitesize

Not Going To Uni
Online apprenticeship guide
www.notgoingtouni.co.uk

StudentBeans
Website dedicated to student deals, discounts and money-saving ideas
www.studentbeans.com/uk

MoneySavingExpert
All sorts of advice for parents and children about money, utilities, insurance etc
www.MoneySavingExpert.com

General dad blogs and websites

@DIYDaddy
www.DadLabs.com
www.huntermovement.com
www.daddilife.com
www.thedadsnet.com
www.fatherhoodinstitute.org

Source Credits

Milestone 1	'Fathers and Their Impact on Children's Well-Being'
Milestone 2	www.madeformums.com/baby/survey-shows-new-dads-frightened-of-holding-their-babies/
Milestone 5	www.independent.ie/life/family/parenting/david-colemans-simple-rules-on-seeing-eyetoeye-with-our-teens-35439636.html
Milestone 6	New York University study
	Marquette University, USA
Milestone 42	*British Journal of Educational Psychology*
	'Why Fathers Matter To Their Children's Literacy'
Milestone 49	Mark Williams, author of *Daddy Blues*
Milestone 52	Daddilife/Deloitte Millennial Dad Study 2019
Milestone 60	Survey by the UK Halifax Building Society
	'CHILDWISE Monitor Report'
Milestone 61	Archives of Pediatric and Adolescent Medicine
Milestone 63	Matthew Moreton, Managing Director at Compare and Recycle
Milestone 67	'Dumbs and Dad' study
15 facts	National Institute of Child Health and Human Development
	Journal of Applied Developmental Psychology
	University of Central London
	'Fathers and Their Impact on Children's Well-Being'
	Psychological Science
	https://www.cell.com/cell-reports/fulltext/S2211-1247(18)30404-2
Milestone 72	Common Sense Media
Milestone 76	Amy Przeworski
Milestone 79	Sainsburys Bank
Milestone 88	NSPCC study in 2016
Milestone 91	www.MoneySavingExpert.com
Milestone 92	Legal & General 2018
Milestone 96	ONS (Office for National Statistics Survey)
	www.ons.gov.uk/peoplepopulationandcommunity/populationandmigration/populationestimates/articles/milestonesjourneyingintoadulthood/2019-02-18
Milestone 99	Survey by Civitas
	US study from the journal *Social Science and Medicine*

Index

attention seeking   120, 154–5

babysitters   44, 102–3
bath time   34–5
bicycles   100–1
birth experience   4–5
body image   160–1
bonding   7, 10, 12, 24, 28–9, 35, 175, 224
boundaries, with adult kids   214–15
boyfriend/girlfriend, meeting   186–7
bullying   136, 142–3
bunking off school   168

careers   180–1, 202–5
children, having more   72–3
chores   172–3
communication   38–9, 48–9, 86–7, 150, 175
    with adult kids   214–15
    serious talks   156–7
crawling   62
curfew   158–9

death   93, 98–9
development   66–7
    crawling and walking   62–3
    and games   36–7
    head raising   26–7
    reflexes   40–1
    response to own name   56–7
differences, from mothers   150–1
divorce   184–5

dress, inappropriate   154–5
driving
    dad as taxi   174–5
    new baby home   8–9
    teaching teen   194–5
drugs   178–9
drunkenness of child   169

empty nests   208–11
eye contact, with baby   10–11

family business   204–5
feeding   12–13, 30–1, 33, 60–1, 94–5
fertility   74–5
fighting with siblings   134–5
finances, student   196–7
first aid   82–3
fitness for dads   75, 138–9
flying   88–9
football   124–5
friends   116–17, 118–19, 154
further education   198–9

games, for babies   36–7
gap years   200–1
girlfriend/boyfriend, meeting   186–7
godfathers   220–1
goodbye, saying   45
grandchildren   215, 222–3
grandparents   21

head, raising baby's   26–7
holding your baby   6–7
holidays, school   140–1
hormones   162–3

illnesses, childhood 76–9

jobs, first 202–3
jokes 122–3

leave, paternity/maternity 24
legal age 192–3

marriage 46–7, 50–1, 54–5
    kids' 192, 218–19
midlife crisis 216–17
misbehaviour, adolescent 164–5,
    182–3
months, speaking in 42
moving, out of/back into the
        family home 206–7,
        212–13
music 188–9

names 14–15, 56–7
nappies 22–3
nights out 44–5
nurseries 18–19

online safety 148–9
overprotection 119

parents' evening 144–5
parties
    birthday 84–5
    teenage 176–7
paternity leave 24–5
pets 92–3, 96–7
phones, first 136–7
photos of your baby 58–9
pocket money 130–1
police, trouble with the 179
politics 190–1
postnatal depression 104–5
potty training 70–1

pubs 64–5
punishment, of teenager 182–3

questions from your child 126–9

reading to your child 90–1
rebellion 154
reflexes 40–1
routines 33, 43, 89
rows with teenagers 170–1

safety 82–3, 148–9
school 114–15, 129
    and bullying 142–3
    holidays 140–1
    parents' evening 144–5
    school reports 146–7
    struggling with 166–8
    teams 132–3
    see also further education
shyness 118–19
siblings, fights with 134–5
skills, dad 108–9
sleep 25, 32–3, 35, 55, 173
social media 58, 148–9,
        160, 215
swearing 120–1
swimming 28

tantrums 86–7
teething 52–3
time for children 106–7, 110–11,
        151
transporters, baby 16–17

visitors, first 20–1
vomit 30–1

walking 62
wills, preparing 80–1

About the author

Rob Kemp is the author of the best-selling *Expectant Dad's Survival Guide* (Vermillion). He began writing about fatherhood when he became an expectant dad in 2003. Already established as the senior writer for *Men's Health* magazine, he was well accustomed to probing experts for advice, putting their insight into layman's terms and then passing it on to readers in an entertaining but down-to-earth style. As a result his writing about fatherhood in a popular *Men's Health* column soon became a labour of love. His well-received articles on the trials and tribulations of becoming a new dad were soon followed by hands-on advice features in a number of parenting titles including *Pregnancy, Baby & You* and *Junior*. He became editor-at-large for the UK's number one dad mag – *FQ* (*Father's Quarterly*) – writing, commissioning and editing practical advice for new fathers and soon-to-be-dads. He regularly contributes fatherhood-focused features to a variety of publications and websites including the *Telegraph, Boots Parenting, Amazon Parents*, the *Guardian, Sainsbury's Fresh Ideas, Daddilife* (as @expectantdad), *The DadClub* and *Little London*. He has spoken at parenting events including the Mumsnet event, BumpFest. His work for *Men's Health* magazine has been syndicated throughout the world and he's made many radio and TV appearances speaking on men's issues and parenting topics.